PRESS

C. A. PRESS

FIND YOUR INNER RED SHOES

Born in Argentina, Mariela Dabbah is an award-winning best-selling author, thought-leader, corporate consultant, and media contributor on issues of education, career development and empowerment with a focus on Latinos. She's a sought-after international speaker and corporate trainer who has inspired diverse audiences to take the steps needed to fulfill their dreams. Dabbah is a frequent guest on CNN, Univision, Telemundo, Fox News, and all the major English and Spanish networks.

In 2009 she created Latinos in College, a nonprofit organization to help Latino students in the U.S. find everything they need to succeed in college. In 2012, after the publication of the Spanish-language edition of this book, she launched the Red Shoe Movement, an initiative that encourages women to wear red shoes to work on Tuesdays to signal their support for other women's career advancement. The goal is to move the needle on female representation at the highest levels of all types of organizations.

Aside from having published six books of nonfiction, Dabbah is also a fiction writer whose stories have been published in literary magazines and online. Her first book of short stories *Cuentos de Nuevos Aires y Buena York* (Metafrasta, 2006) has received wide public and critical acclaim and her first novel will be published soon. She lives in New York.

FIND YOUR INNER RED SHOES

*Step into Your Own
Style of Success*

Mariela Dabbah

C. A. PRESS
Penguin Group (USA)

C. A. PRESS
Published by the Penguin Group
Penguin Group (USA) Inc., 375 Hudson Street,
New York, New York 10014, USA

USA | Canada | UK | Ireland | Australia | New Zealand | India | South Africa | China
Penguin Books Ltd, Registered Offices: 80 Strand, London WC2R 0RL, England
For more information about the Penguin Group visit penguin.com

First published by C. A. Press, a member of Penguin Group (USA) Inc., 2012
This English-language edition published 2013

Copyright © Mariela Dabbah, 2012
Translation copyright © Mariela Dabbah, 2013
All rights reserved. No part of this product may be reproduced, scanned, or distributed in any
printed or electronic form without permission. Please do not participate in or encourage piracy of
copyrighted materials in violation of the author's rights. Purchase only authorized editions.

Translation by Karen Tawil

ISBN 978-0-14-242690-6

Printed in the United States of America
10 9 8 7 6 5 4 3 2 1

While the author has made every effort to provide accurate telephone numbers and Internet
addresses at the time of publication, neither the publisher nor the author assumes any responsibility
for errors or for changes that occur after publication. Further, publisher does not have any control
over and does not assume any responsibility for author or third-party Web sites or their content.

ALWAYS LEARNING   PEARSON

To my mother, Gabriela Abeles,
to who I owe so much of my own success

To my friend Susan Landon,
who has supported my writing for years
behind the scenes

To Arturo Poiré,
because only an official dedication can express
how significant his contributions have been

Contents

CONTENTS

PART THREE
Moving Ahead! Plain Sailing

"Everything passes and everything remains
But we can only pass
Pass making paths
Pathways over the sea
(...)
Wayfarer your footsteps are the path and nothing more
Wayfarer there is no path, the path is forged as you tread
By treading you make the path, and when glancing back
You see the path that you'll never tread again
Wayfarer there is no path but waves on the sea"

—*"Caminante no hay camino"*
by Joan Manuel Serrat
(based on Antonio Machado's
homonymous poem)

Introduction

I wrote this book with the intention of not creating another typical self-help book. You know what I'm talking about, the kind that promises a magic potion that will change your life. Those books you read enthused at first, only to realize their strategy isn't going to work for you. Yours is a different case altogether. Of course, it can't be otherwise. Your case is special, only you walk in your shoes. So instead of reading these pages trying to copy the formula that worked for someone else, I'd like you to read them trying to find clues to help you design your own journey. A journey that is good for you and only you. It's best to be open to the ideas I'll be presenting as well as to the voices of several others, who are mostly women. Select the ones whose journey or individual style appeals to you most. And do the same with the specific tools I'll share with you. These are strategies and concepts that worked for me and many other women who were able to find a successful path that lead to fulfillment and happiness. It is equally important to approach these newly identified wishes and goals with ease. Sometimes, when we suddenly realize what we want, we become anxious about time lost or annoyed with ourselves. To make up for it we try skipping over stages which, in turn, leads to greater frustration.

You should think about professional and personal success as a journey, not a destination; the journey each of us builds in order to experience what really pleases us. So if this book helps you find out what you want for yourself professionally, it will also help you find ways to align your wishes with actions you must perform to fulfill them. That same alignment is a success in and of itself, and it will make you feel more fulfilled than you did before, when you didn't know what you wanted professionally.

But let's start from the very beginning.

The word *success* derives from the Latin *succedere* which means "come after" and "accomplishment of desired end."

And if we are going to discuss success, we need to talk about its opposite, failure, for it's hard to fully capture the meaning of one without the other.

The word *failure* comes from the old French word *faillir*, which derives from the Latin *fallere*: "to cause to fall" or "to disappoint."

For each person, success, that accomplishment of desired end, takes a different shape. It's a journey on which each of us embarks with our own singular style.

When we understand success in these terms, as embarking on a journey, a satisfactory way out for each one of us, it's possible to move away from the simplistic *success* and *failure* dichotomy, which can ultimately create a suffocating "no way out" situation. On the other hand, when considering success as a destination (a goal to achieve) as opposed to failure (and considering that its parameters are defined by society, your parents, coworkers or anyone other than you), if you don't reach that destination, you're doomed to failure. For example, in American society one of the most common stereotypes is equating success with having certain material things: a house, a car, etc. Maybe it's more satisfying for you to live in the city, in a rented apartment, getting around by public transport, and having the chance to enjoy cultural outings each evening. But if you stick to the conventional idea of success (like most people do), even if you're satisfied and happy with your city life, you'll continue struggling to purchase a home in the suburbs.

Lucía Ballas-Traynor, cofounder of MamasLatinas.com, a website that focuses on Hispanic women's needs, speaks about her own definition of success and leadership: "I'll never forget the time when I told one of my bosses that as a woman I felt the way I was being treated, and the level of respect I was afforded, was different from that of the *boys club*. He answered, 'when you walk into a room, there are three strikes against you: you're a woman, you're Hispanic and you're short.' I feel that in our business, men set the rules and we must adapt to their definition of leadership. I left a few jobs because I wasn't willing to do what it took to reach the next level. To continue being true to myself, it's more important to strike a balance between my personal and professional life than making progress in my career. Many men think that success is always related to their ego and the next promotion. Since they're the established group in leadership positions, leadership is based on male genetic markers, and I'm convinced that even if females are promoted and break certain barriers, their genetic makeup is different. Unless we redefine the notion of leadership to embrace women too, this will continue to be a man's world."

Once you understand that success is what works best for each person, you'll be able to shake off the stress that ensues when meeting goals you haven't set for yourself, and that most likely don't even make you happy. Just like Lucía did when she left certain jobs throughout her career because they didn't fit her definition of success.

How Does It Work?

If you follow me through a brief digression on identity formation and how it shapes us, you'll get a sense of certain assumptions this book is based on. As a newborn, you as a person are still "undetermined" because you haven't created your own identity. This primal need to find comfort in another human to affirm that we exist begins at birth. You may know, for instance, that babies seek to connect to their mother's body, warmth, pulse, and gaze; they need to be touched, cuddled, and rocked to develop abilities such as empathy. That initial recognition required from others to endorse your existence carries certain predeterminations. In psychology these are defined as the concepts and ideas that precede any conscious decision by an individual; the kind of subconscious, ancestral, genetic or social influences that have nothing to do with the person's own will but with what he/she is born with and what is instilled in them very early on. (Think about the dreams and expectations that your family had for you when you were in your mother's womb. Who they thought you'd become and what they expected you to like.)

It's through the process of detaching yourself from those predetermined notions that you become a person. Once you're able to detach, you're open to the possibility of learning and creating. If you find your own personal style, you may pursue your journey as someone with an identity of your own, and not one established by others.

Even before grabbing at the chance to pave your own way—or finding the way out as I mentioned before—there must be a break from what you identify with. That fear of separation is the natural fear of failure we all have when breaking away from family mandates. It's that fear of rejecting the ideals our family and ancestors had in store for us; that fear of being different from our parents.

Consider this: children want what their parents, grandparents or caregivers want. Naturally, they still can't know what they want for themselves. This ability to identify your own desire becomes possible when disidentification from the mother/father figure, and the wishes they hold for you, occurs. The process of disidentification from those key figures in order to identify with your own wishes (that initial failure) yields the chance of building a way out: *exit* → *success*. Therefore, failure isn't really an outcome, but a starting point.

Let's say your parents always pushed you to become a lawyer and you never managed to define your own dreams (you wanted to be a painter), and for many years you mixed up your wishes with theirs. You would say to yourself, "I want to be a lawyer; when I become a lawyer I will have achieved success." You automatically followed all the necessary steps to graduate from law school and then started practicing law. You have loads of clients and are good at what you do because you have trained and prepared yourself for years. But, for some reason, you are not satisfied with your work.

Little by little you realize you want to be a painter and that the only time you really feel happy is at painting class or on the evenings you spend at home painting. One day, it just dawns on you that you were never interested in becoming a lawyer. You went to law school because it was your parents' dream. First, you'll probably experience mixed feelings of pain for the time lost, followed by a sense of relief now knowing why your work doesn't feel rewarding, although you earn good money and have a sizeable clientele. You're facing a break, a form of failure, which may cause feelings of unrest and anguish at first.

In other words, you'll be undergoing the process of "disidentifying" yourself from those predetermined rules others consciously or subconsciously imposed on you. Only then, and by reaching this point of failure, will you be able to embark on your path. Sometimes you need professional assistance to go through these moments and in the following chapters I'll also offer you tools to help you first identify those predetermined labels and then work on disidentifying yourself, and, finally, build the success that fits your own style.

For the purpose of this book, I'll assume you're looking for greater professional satisfaction, and your search includes achieving both material as well as social recognition for your professional contributions. I'll assume that to attain these goals you're willing to reflect, do some introspection, as well as listen to the stories of other women who have achieved success and hold important positions within their industries or interest areas. Success is marked by an ability to make decisions that will impact your future, as well as a capacity to exert influence in order to achieve both personal or group-oriented goals.

Keep in mind that the factors I've taken into account when speaking about successful women are based on the capitalistic society I live in. My suggestion to you is not to get stuck trying to replicate any person's story because each of these women made it in their own way, as best they could, using what they had readily available. Each built their own experience, something you cannot teach or learn. You have yours and I have mine. You may live your experience in a certain way and I may go through that same experience in a completely different manner. I can certainly tell you what worked for me, which is what these women did when I interviewed them. Most importantly, you must remember to build your own unique story, in your own style, with your own special traits, without becoming upset if you're not able to be like this person or the next. It's your life after all.

YOUR VOICE THROUGH SOCIAL NETWORKS

"Success is liking yourself."
—*Martina Caracoche, advertising student, via Facebook*

When I think of the successful women I know, regardless of whether they're artists, own their own business, work for a large corporation, a nonprofit organization or the private sector, they all have these traits in common.

> They're passionate about what they do
> They derive great satisfaction from their work
> They're sure they can achieve what they set out to do (self-confidence)
> They're ambitious and have been so since they were young although they didn't know "that" was called ambition
> They're not afraid of challenges
> They've developed a sound network of contacts throughout their careers
> They've had numerous supporters, often informal, and formal mentors and sponsors
> They follow their own definition of success

Research backs my observations. In the book *Successful Professional Women of the Americas* (Edward Elgar Publishing Ltd, 2006), coauthored by Jo Ann Duffy, Suzy Fox, Ann Gregory, Terri R.Lituchy, Silvia Inés Monserrat, Miguel R. Olivas-Luján, Betty Jane Punnett, and Neusa Maria Bastos F. Santos, the authors conducted wide research on the subject of success and women in Latin America, the U.S., and Canada. They found that successful women shared some of the following qualities: self-efficacy, i.e., the belief that one is able to serve successfully in a specific field; the belief that success and failure are more related to their own actions than to external factors; and a preference for challenging tasks that require extra work.

Simultaneously, the researchers correlated the women's cultural values with personality traits and discovered that, in spite of some differences according to region, typically in all countries researched, successful women:

> ➢ Were moderately individualistic. This trait is typical in countries like the U.S. but not in Latin America where a collectivistic focus is the norm.
> ➢ Displayed moderate risk aversion compared to the Latin American high-risk aversion trend. This differs from the U.S. where people tend to take on more risks.
> ➢ Had little acceptance for the so-called "power distance," the idea that power is a right bestowed through lineage. In contrast to the U.S. where anyone can be successful regardless of their family background, most Latin Americans accept the restraints of their social class which results in low levels of social mobility in the region.

The idea behind this book is not to make you feel you must improve, change or acquire what you don't already have, but to offer you strategic distinctions to help you realize your own goals. Throughout these pages, choose what you find useful and set aside what's not. The more aware you are of what you want and what you're worth—this includes knowing your strengths, weaknesses, style, and the image you project—the more possibilities you'll have to attract what you want. Within this insightful process, we'll also touch upon personality and cultural traits which can be modulated (like raising and lowering the volume) according to the environment you're in.

Often, when I present before groups of employees within large multinational corporations, someone will ask me, "But, why should

I stop being who I am to go to work? Why can't I keep my personality and culture?"

The answer is pretty complex. On the one hand, they hired you for being who you are, for knowing what you know, and for your potential. The idea is not to abandon who you are and become another person, but to tap into your unique perspective (made up in part by your cultural background) to enhance the company, organization or industry you serve. Yet, every time a large group of individuals gets together to work or have fun, each one makes concessions for the benefit of the group. The key is never involving your identity in those concessions but tapping into who you are in order to achieve your goals.

Consider this as an example: if you were in Japan and went to a local family's home for five o'clock tea, you would surely take off your shoes when stepping indoors since it's customary. And you probably wouldn't feel as if you were not being yourself for doing so, but respecting Japanese tradition and adapting to the circumstance. Something similar happens in the workplace. If your communication style is excessively passionate, you might find it hard to communicate with executives who typically favor a softer, more analytic style. On the other hand, if you lower the volume on your style while keeping the passion, you'll have many opportunities to sit at the decision-making table.

Before I go on, I'd like to credit Lucía Ballas-Traynor for coining the term "modulate" as used above when, as Director of *People en Español*, she commissioned a study called Hispanic Opinion Tracker (HOT) to learn about how Hispanic women adjust their cultural temperature (being more or less "Latina") according to the role they're in. And since this book attempts to guide you to places typically populated by men, I thought it was important to include the voice of Arturo Poiré, a man who has worked relentlessly at opening doors for women and minorities at some of the largest corporations in the U.S.

Throughout the book you'll find "Arturo Poiré's Corner," where I'll be sharing parts of my lengthy conversations with this dear friend and coauthor of *The Latino Advantage in the Workplace* (Sphinx Publishing, 2006). Given his background in sociology, his MBA degree, and his experience in human resources serving as a top executive in Citigroup and Marsh & McLennan Companies, Arturo offers a wise and valuable point of view. And he recently accepted a new challenge by moving from the U.S. to Sweden to serve as Head of Talent Management for the large global tech company, Ericsson.

One more thing before we get started. I'd like for you to know the story behind those sassy heels on the cover which began the Red Shoe Movement and which you can read more about on page 227. While trying to envision the cover for this book, along with a symbol most women would equate power with femininity with, the red stilettos immediately came to mind. I wanted the image to convey the idea that you as woman can reach any level you aspire to and on your own terms. There's no need to adopt anybody else's style to reach your goals. Let those iconic heels serve as a reminder that only you can walk in your own shoes and that it behooves you to respect your own particular style. Let the journey begin.

FIND
YOUR INNER
RED SHOES

PART ONE

Understanding Where You Come from and Where You're Headed

Chapter 1

What Do Successful Women
Have in Common?

Famous Women Speak: Roselyn Sánchez

Born in Puerto Rico, the actress Roselyn Sánchez started out her career as a teen model before she moved to the U.S. without her parents in search of acting opportunities. She was the first Latina to be cast in the legendary soap opera "As the World Turns," and after appearing in minor roles on television and the big screen, she received her big break in Hollywood costarring in *Rush Hour 2* with Jackie Chan and Chris Tucker. In 2008 Roselyn was awarded an Alma Award for her role in the CBS series "Without a Trace" and she's currently filming two feature films. In both, she'll star as two exceptional women: Rosa Helena Fergusson, the teacher who taught Gabriel García Márquez how to read (based on the book *La Maestra y el Nóbel* by Beatriz Parga), and Doña Felisa Rincón de Gautier, the mayoress of San Juan, Puerto Rico who was reelected five times.

Q: *What prompted you to leave Puerto Rico to pursue your dream of studying acting in New York? Who encouraged you? Did it generate any conflicts with your parents? As a woman, what was this experience like?*

A: My decision to leave when I was twenty-one was spontaneous, though

I had always thought about it since I was young. I always wanted to develop a career in arts, and I admit I always visualized myself outside Puerto Rico. My country is beautiful, my family, and good friends are there. My childhood was perfectly normal; I went to college in Puerto Rico, worked for a television station there, so everything seemed to suggest my professional life would unfold on the island. But once I won a beauty pageant in the U.S. representing Puerto Rico, I decided to follow my dream and move to New York to study musical drama. It was a rash, but clear-cut decision. At first, my parents didn't agree to it because they wanted me to finish college, but I had already made up my mind. It was very hard in the beginning because although New York is a dynamic and wonderful city, it could also be a monster for a young, naïve girl who didn't speak English fluently and was only guided by her angel and a great dream. I grew a lot as a woman. In three years I learned what I hadn't learned in twenty-one! It was a pleasant surprise knowing I could fall in love with the idea of being independent. To bet on myself.

Q: *What motherly advice encouraged you to pursue your goal? What did you learn in Puerto Rico?*

A: The most valuable piece of advice my mother offered me was: "Don't ever let anyone cut off your wings." I always use her valuable advice as my guiding star. A friend once told me: "If I had the chance to live in New York, I would never sleep; there are so many options, Roselyn, so much to do, so many cultural offerings . . . make the most of every second." The nicest thing I learned from my country was patriotism. Feeling proud of telling everybody wherever I went 'I'm Puerto Rican.' We are a very proud people, proud of our roots and our talent.

Q: *What does success mean to you? What gives you great satisfaction?*

A: The most valuable thing success gives me is the platform and convening power to help others. I love the philanthropic work I'm lucky enough to do thanks to the opportunity God gave me to be acknowledged. Doors open up faster when ideas arise and I'm able to make things happen. I love my profession, I'm passionate about acting, singing, dancing, and can't imagine doing anything else.

Q: *What do you learn from your female characters?*

A: The women I portray have taught me to be strong. I've always played the role of educated, independent, intelligent, and strong Latinas. I love them because they're three-dimensional and it's very *chévere* to be trusted with creating a female character; first studying the material and then assigning them traits of women I admire.

Q: *Was there a time you wanted to give up your dream? Who helped you remain focused?*

A: I've never wanted to give up, though I admit there are times I get tired of so much rejection and having to constantly fight for recognition. I'm very perseverant and self-confident and I don't like to be told no. They could deny me a hundred times, but I'm always certain I'll be getting a yes soon enough. I have God's favor, and those who fight always attain victory, even if it's not in the way we wanted. I can't complain. I've always been blessed with work, people's love, and admiration from my loved ones, friends, and followers.

Have you ever wondered how you get to be a famous actress or artist? A president of a country or of a multimillion dollar corporation? A woman who manages a large foundation or employs hundreds of people in their own company? How about those kinds of moms who hold high-pressure jobs, have children they adore, and seem to manage it all with great ease? Who are these women and what's their secret?

When I've been asked, "Which of your personality traits do you attribute to your success?" I often answer using adjectives shared by all those who are successful at what they do: I'm perseverant, I don't quit easily, I'm positive, I trust myself.

I'd like you to think that you probably have these same traits as well or you wouldn't be reading a book on success. The secret is to recognize you have such traits and channel them toward achieving your goals.

THE VOICE OF EXPERIENCE

"In a 2010 Hispanic Opinion Tracker (HOT) study we asked Hispanic women to define success. While Latinas checked the 'money' category, non-Latinas checked 'happy.' I think this is due in part to the fact that Latinas are relatively new to the workforce, they're young, profession-oriented, and the majority are happy to have a career. But once you've been working for some time (and Anglo-Saxon women have been in the workforce for two or three generations now), you realize success is not just about having money and a degree, but also about being happy."

—*Lucía Ballas-Traynor, cofounder of MamasLatinas.com*

What Successful Women Are Not—Afraid

For many of us, the list of fears we've grown up with, and still keep, is longer than the Mississippi River. And sometimes we're not even aware of them. Read the list below and try to remember if at any given time in your life you've experienced one or more of the following fears:

- Of failure
- Of letting your parents down (both or either one of them)
- Of success
- Of not living up to expectations

> ➢ Of being rejected by your family once you've attained success (educational, financial)
> ➢ Of surpassing your mom or dad's educational level
> ➢ Of being physically apart from your family
> ➢ Of not being able to strike a balance between your personal and professional life
> ➢ Of speaking in public
> ➢ Of speaking about your achievements and appearing conceited
> ➢ Of asking for what you want (without expecting others to guess)
> ➢ Of not being 100% ready for that wonderful opportunity you've been offered
> ➢ Of wishing for material things (perhaps you were raised to be detached from the material world)

It took me several years to overcome a good deal of these fears, and I still struggle with them on a daily basis. I was raised by a traditional and well-off family in Argentina. My father is an orthopedic surgeon, and my mother taught kindergarten. She was nine courses short of receiving a degree in psychology when my older brother was born. She abandoned her career and stopped working until many years later when she started managing the men's clothing stores our family owned. Mom showed us how her incredible energy, organizational skills, and the pleasant demeanor she displayed at home, also made her an excellent manager at work. She was loved and respected by her employees, suppliers, and clients.

This change in attitude toward her career came too late to serve as a model for me. One of my greatest fears during my teenage years and early twenties was outdoing my mother by completing my university studies. I remember it as if it were today; how hard it was to sit for those final exams. Attaining that degree was like betraying my mom who had abandoned her university studies to take care of her children.

The other great fear back then was not being able to find my own place as an independent woman without a man to support me (my dad's dream). Since my father was always someone with a high profile in our country, I wanted to get out from under his shadow and reap my own success. I overcame the first fear acknowledging and accepting my responsibility, and, above all, understanding that completing my university studies was the best way to honor what I wanted for my future.

The second one took many more years to overcome. Though not having models to follow can often be a much harder place for kids to start from, many children of well-known people can also find it difficult to set their own course. When your identity is forged in connection to a successful parent, there seems to be little space left to build a name for yourself. Becoming my own person, with my own achievements, values, and dreams seemed like a long shot. Especially without relying on a husband to contribute to my new identity.

It's possible that fears like these are already history to you. But it's also pretty possible that you're still suffering from certain fears either consciously or unconsciously. Yet, the reason why I began this chapter discussing traits that successful women don't display is because they've somehow conquered those fears and uncertainties while toning down the negative from their lives.

This doesn't mean they're not concerned when faced with the unknown, or afraid of not living up to what others expect of them, but that they use such concerns as stimuli to launch the next adventure. It's likely they're also aware of these fears and seek professional help so that they can continue brushing them away when they appear. To a certain extent, all the women I interviewed were able to break free from the predeterminations of their past and find their own style. To quote Argentine psychoanalyst Ingrid El-licker, "They considered what they have lived so far as destiny and the future as free will."

The Power of Language

Typically, structural fears originate in our relationships with our parents and experiences we lived as kids and teenagers. Now, as adults, we are conditioned by our history to believe that what we fear is as real as the chair you're sitting in.

But consider this: when fear of failure paralyzes you and prevents you from making decisions, unless you have a physical disability, you're mainly paralyzed in terms of language. Nobody tied your legs to a rope and that rope to a stone to stop you from moving. The expression "I am paralyzed" is just that—an expression containing three words. And that expression (or any other: "I'm stuck," "I can't do it," "I'm afraid") is greatly responsible for you being in the same place year after year when you'd rather be elsewhere. This is an example of the enormous power of language in not just describing a situation, person or object, but in creating conditions, situations, and events.

Here's another example. When you make arrangements with someone for lunch, you are creating an engagement, an event that was inexistent a few minutes ago. You are creating it in language. If you don't honor the appointment, your behavior will carry consequences. If you fail to honor your commitments several times, your reputation is at stake because people will believe you can't keep your word!

Something similar happens with fears. First, circumstances are experienced and then your words create a reality. You are really afraid of failure. (This is most likely your fear of doing something different than what's expected of you.) You feel it in your guts every time you start a project you don't feel prepared for. The best thing is to acknowledge that such a reality has been created for you by others and that you're capable of creating another reality more in tune with your own wishes. You can start by saying to yourself and those around you, "I love challenges. I know I can do it," and, little by little, use language to create a reality that better fits your aspirations. In the next chapter we'll talk more in depth about this subject.

♥   ♥   ♥   ♥   ♥

How to Shake Off Fears That Paralyze You

If you've been burdened with a fear that paralyzes you when accepting a promising opportunity, the inevitable first step is to identify it. Remember what I told you in the introduction—only after you've become aware of what you're identifying with can you later "disidentify" and detach from it.

Look at the list I included at the beginning of the chapter and put an "x" by the fears you have experienced or still feel. Then add any others you may have that are not on that list. The next step is to disidentify from those messages. Let them fall. Perhaps you'll need the support of a psychologist or some coaching to shake off certain messages. For now, observe and reflect on them. In other words, don't just think about each specific fear, but reflect on them. Look, analyze, and think of yourself through the perspective of that fear. Feel how that deep-seated fear creeps into you.

Start taking small steps to break away from old fears. For example, if you're afraid of failure, volunteer to do something you would normally refuse. Experience the process of researching a new subject, socializing with people outside of your regular circle, or training in a different discipline. As you gain confidence, you'll start taking on greater risks.

Any time you feel overwhelmed by your fears, deconstruct the expression into words, analyze it, and then analyze yourself. Examine your reaction vis-à-vis the situation and recognize that if you're able to find new words to talk about the situation, you'll slowly create a new reality. And keep in mind Ingrid Ellicker's words: try to consider that destiny (what you've inherited from your family) belongs to the past, and the future lies in your hands. You may use your free will to determine what journey appeals to you.

Viewing the Future

Now let's move on to what those women who inspire us *do* have. Beyond the list I gave you in the introduction, these women can see themselves in the future. They know what they want and are actively involved in letting others know about it and attaining it. They're fully aware that each decision will impact their future and are diligent decision makers. They struggle to align their actions with their own desires (with an emphasis on "own" because these are different from the wishes others may have had in store for them).

Let me ask you: what do you dream of being five, ten or twenty years from now? What do you want your legacy to be? What's your personal dream, the one you hold for yourself, and not what others dreamed for you?

The truth is many of us are not used to these types of exercises. For two reasons: first, because as a child, if your family pushed you to study, chances are they led you toward more traditional careers, taking up the family business, or, like me, studying anything I wanted as long as I studied. In other words, your parents, grandparents, and uncles pushed you to go along with the wishes they had in store for you. With ideals they themselves weren't able to realize that were passed on, like a family jewel, to the next generation.

> **YOUR VOICE THROUGH SOCIAL NETWORKS**
>
> "I loved astronomy and I always dreamed of being an astronaut. When the movie *Space Camp* came out I only wanted to go to Florida to visit the Space Camp. But money was always an issue so I never got to go. Up to this day I become very excited whenever there's a space shuttle mission and I try to watch takeoffs and landings on television. I even follow some astronauts on Twitter!"　　*—Shirley Limongy via LinkedIn*

At my house, like in the homes of many professional families, not going to college was not an option. The only option was what specialty I wanted to study. Interestingly enough, my older brother never had that choice. Instead of following his dream of becoming an aircraft pilot, he had to follow in my father's footsteps and graduated as an orthopedic surgeon. (Similar to the example of the lawyer in the introduction.)

My younger sister and I were able to choose our careers not because my father suddenly became more lenient, but because as women (and back then) he expected us to get married and have husbands to support us. This was certainly a clear family mandate which took me years to detach from. Therefore, it was completely meaningless what career we decided to pursue. It's true things have changed a bit since then, but in many countries they haven't changed that much. The concept of helping children explore several career options, and to dream who they'd like to be when they grow up, is not widespread enough.

Another reason you might not have a clear picture of what you want for yourself can sometimes have to do with where your parents and grandparents come from geographically. For instance, the relative instability and incidence of the unexpected in Latin America renders mid- and long-term planning almost null among people brought up in the region. The same is true for people who come from areas affected by ongoing wars, with social, political, and economic unrest.

On the other hand, in a stable country with a capitalist economy like the U.S., where success, competitiveness, and attaining material possessions are very much in synch, there's a strong incentive for planning and individual fulfillment. Children and teenagers are exposed early on to an assortment of professional options through school programs and extracurricular activities. Particularly, middle-class Anglo-Saxon parents encourage their children to dream, explore, and discover interests, and their lives are pretty much planned from kindergarten to college graduation. And, of course, once they embark on their careers they go on to fulfill their professional goals.

The majority of successful women I interviewed, regardless of where they were brought up, had this type of experience. Thanks to that father, mother, grandmother or grandfather who pushed them to think about a bright future, to pursue their dreams through education, and to get involved in areas they were interested in or passionate about.

If you haven't done it yet, I invite you to do so now. Take a few minutes to start imagining how you see yourself in the future.

♥   ♥   ♥   ♥   ♥

A Spiritual Spa

Make yourself some coffee and sit somewhere with a great view. I love the view of the Hudson River close to home, but you can choose a park, the beach or the twenty-fifth floor of a building with a spectacular view. Obviously, it depends on where you live and your own creativity to find that inspiring place.

Take a look at that magnificent view in front of you, inhale and exhale a few times, disconnect from work and your concerns, and let your mind drift. Don't fix your eyes on any given point. Then start focusing on your dream. How do you see yourself five years from now? How far up would you like to go in your career? What lifestyle would you feel satisfied with? What type of influence would you like to exert?

As you build the idea of this woman into the future, try to imagine all the details: your home, family, type of work-related activities, location, office, employees, etc. The more detailed the dream, the better.

You may have to repeat this exercise several times until you're clear about what you want. Sometimes, because we've been disconnected from our wishes for so long (or maybe we've never even considered this question) it's hard to distinguish what we really want for ourselves and what others want from us. Don't let fears get in the way.

When you feel you've been able to capture the description that best relates to your innermost wish, write it down so that you can go back to it from time to time to make sure your decisions are bringing you closer to your dream. It's also important to articulate this wish so that your bosses and other coworkers may help you accomplish it.

♠   ♠   ♠   ♠   ♠

Dreaming About Your Future

I don't know how much you believe in the impact of visualization. Oftentimes, a subject becomes trendy and concepts get simplified to the point of totally offsetting its intended results. Something similar occurred recently with *The Secret* by Rhonda Byrne (Atria Books, 2006) and the subsequent comercialization of books specializing in the law of attraction theme. As a result, many people were led to believe that by visualizing what they want, by drawing it or saying it out loud often enough, it would magically appear at their doorstep. Unfortunately, that's not how things really work.

There are virtually hundreds of scientific experiments that support the connection between our intention and the results attained. Though it has yet to be proven that if you sit down and wish for a million dollars, the money will magically appear in your bank account. These experiments are much subtler, where scientists—using machines, bacteria, plants, and healing wounds for example—measure human beings' influence on naturally occurring random results. These machines called RNGs *random number generators*, are used by scientists worldwide to study the existence of powers such as telepathy, long distance vision, and more. For over ten years, Princeton University has been conducting the Global Consciousness Project whereby these random number generating machines "flip a coin" to see whether it falls heads or tails at a rate of two-hundred times per second. The hypothesis they are attempting to confirm is that a universal conscience spread throughout the earth exists, and when significant events occur, such as the 9/11 terrorist attacks or the Indian Ocean tsunami, these generators show patterns that are not likely to occur in random sequences.

THE VOICE OF EXPERIENCE

"Ever since I was a child I was ambitious. Even back when I was in first grade and was asked what I wanted to be when I grew up I would say, loud and clear, that I wanted to be a diplomat in order to help countries communicate and make progress for the benefit of their people. I

believe my cultural background had a great impact on my ambition given the work ethics the majority of Argentines are brought up with. My desire or ambition to become a diplomat was partly influenced by witnessing social chaos resulting from political conflicts. And though I may not be a diplomat in a strict government policy sense today, I've always acted as one in my career, establishing relationships between stakeholders for the benefit of the organization and the public I serve."
—*Carla Dodds, Senior Director, Multicultural Marketing, Walmart Stores*

If you're interested in pursuing the subject further, you may explore several books[1] or access www.theintentionexperiment.com and take part in the numerous global intention experiments Lynne McTaggart, author of the book *The Field* (Harper Collins, 2001), conducts each year. These studies demonstrate that when you focus on your intention you may attain incredible results. And in terms of what we've been discussing here, if you're able to define who you are and where you want to be, and you manage to see yourself in the future with all the particulars of the case, you will then be able to focus your attention on doing what it takes to reach that place and to meet the people who can support you. You'll be able to align your words and actions with that intention. Everything you do will be consistent and send off a uniform image of who you are and what you're looking for, and this, in turn, will convey to others ways in which they might help you fulfill your life purpose. Believe it or not, you will attract what you desire as if you were a great magnet.

In nature, it is common for coherent organisms to influence those that are less coherent. Which means that if you practice disciplines like meditation, yoga, martial arts or any other that will

1. *A New Science of Life/Morphic* Resonance, Rupert Sheldrake, Ph.D. Icon Books, 2009.
The Tao of Physics, Fritjof Capra, Ph.D. Shambhala Publications, 1999.
Space, Time and Medicine, Larry Dossey, MD. Shambhala Publications, 1982.
Molecules of Emotion, Candace Pert, Ph.D. Scribner, 1997.
The Quantum Doctor, Amit Goswami, Ph.D. Hampton Roads, 2004.

help you focus, you'll be more likely to impact others with more scattered energies. Perhaps you have noticed this in the presence of beings such as the Dalai Lama, a yoga master, a shaman, someone who does Reiki or any deeply spiritual being. Do you remember how the energy in the room changed when that person walked in? It's fascinating to see the effect these beings have on others. To a great extent, that calmness, that serenity they convey comes from having a high level of inner coherence, i.e., having focused energy and a clear intention. For the majority of these individuals their intention is related to achieving a state of spiritual peace, unity with the whole, transcendence, etc. From them you can learn that when you organize your energy you can then organize your thoughts, your decisions, and your actions; all of which work to pull you toward what you desire.

THE VOICE OF EXPERIENCE

"I visualize my goals. I look five or ten years down the road and then I build a path from my current position. That's how I plan my next steps. But since many roads lead to Rome, you must be flexible because sometimes you must go back one step to take another longer step forward. And in regards to this, it's helped me to remember what my dad used to say. Since my brain examines a decision from so many angles, there comes a point where I get stuck. He taught me to also trust my instincts because whatever decision I make now, is a decision for the next step, not for a lifetime. Knowing that has set me free."
—Cristina Vilella, Marketing Director, McDonald's USA

From the lengthy list of women I spoke to while writing this book, some like Terri D. Austin, Vice President and Chief Diversity Officer at McGraw Hill Companies, use a visualization technique that includes writing down their goals: "I visualize my long term goals and then I write down the short term steps I must take to achieve those goals. For instance, one of my next career goals is to become a media correspondent. My first task in connection with that goal is to publish a book on diversity and inclusion to establish more credibility in the field."

Others like Lucía Ballas-Traynor, the former Director of *People en Español*, visualize their aspirations internally: "They're in my head; I know the plan. For example, when I was hired for this position, I knew that if I didn't achieve the milestones I had laid out for myself, I would look for another job. But I don't write down my goals, I visualize them." Or like Daisy Auger-Domínguez, VP Organizational and Workforce Diversity at Disney ABC Television Group, who first visualizes her goals internally, and then explores her options: "I test out ideas on colleagues, friends, family, and mentors. I share them in small pieces, keeping the subject broad and confidential until I have a clear picture of where I want to go. I'm ultimately open to possibilities."

Whatever the method that works for you, it's important to define your goals (either in writing, orally or mentally). It increases the likelihood of goals becoming real because it offers clarity, which in turn is conveyed down to your decisions, and later on into your actions. It's critical to remain open to possibilities, as Daisy says, but if you don't have a clear idea where you're headed, you may end up making an unnecessary number of detours. If you remember the conversation between Alice and the Cat in Lewis Carroll's *Alice in Wonderland*, you'll clearly see the conflict you face when you're uncertain. The conversation goes like this:

Alice: *. . . I just wanted to ask which way I ought to go.*
Cat: *Well, that depends on where you ought to get to.*
Alice: *Oh, it really doesn't matter, as long as I . . .*
Cat: *Then it really doesn't matter which way you go.*

18

Due to a blend of cultural traits most of us share, we Latinas are particularly predisposed to such detours. We either find it hard to say no when we're asked to do something or we're extremely loyal to our bosses and colleagues. If you haven't defined your professional goals, it's easy to waste time and detour from the course whenever someone asks you to get involved in a project or take on a role that isn't aligned with your own ambitions.

Every now and then I find myself adjusting the course of my sailboat. It's hard to say no when I'm invited to speak at a conference, even though many don't offer compensation. These events can be an opportunity to speak before potential clients. Others allow me to make an impact on the Hispanic community. But due to time restraints, I must constantly assess opportunities in order not to dilute my resources in hundreds of pro bono presentations a year. When I notice I'm accepting too many invitations without pay, I stop and remind myself that this doesn't contribute to my goal of making a living through my work. I remind myself that I can only devote part of my time to pro bono work, otherwise I won't have enough income to continue creating more educational and professional programs to benefit those in need while earning a living. These are common adjustments we all make in the course of doing business, but if I didn't have clear goals in mind, I wouldn't even realize I was headed off course.

What works for me is a blend of tools. For one, psychoanalysis has contributed a space for sustainable growth. If you know anything about Argentine culture, I'm sure it'll come as no surprise that I have a therapist. Argentina has the largest number of psychologists per capita worldwide. The type of psychotherapy I'm involved with is based on language and it allows for a deeper level of understanding not only of myself, but also of my professional work. Many people in high positions consider their psychoanalyst or personal coach as one of the most precious members of their support team.

I've also been practicing transcendental meditation for years. And the truth is my life completely shifts when I go through periods where I'm too busy to meditate. (Sadly, those are the times when I most need it!) My energy scatters, my attention is impaired and everything entails a greater effort. When I'm disciplined and meditate daily, things flow naturally, I experience countless synchronous situations, I meet the right people at the right time; I'm "lucky." It's hard to explain, but that's the way it is. When you sit in silence and allow your mind to remain unattached to thoughts, for a brief moment you experience the source where thoughts arise from, what is known as transcendental consciousness or the unified field. It's the most silent and peaceful level of consciousness. In this state of relaxation your brain works with a much higher level of consistency. I encourage you to start your own meditation routine and see the results for yourself.

What Is Transcendental Meditation?

Transcendental meditation (or TM), is the most well-researched meditation technique. Hundreds of studies have been conducted on it in hundreds of universities and research centers worldwide. Based on the ancient Vedic tradition in India passed on from generation to generation, by 1955 Maharishi Mahesh Yogi (who achieved fame as the guru to The Beatles), introduced transcendental meditation into the contemporary world.

♥ ♥ ♥ ♥ ♥

How to Start a Meditation Practice

Just like there are various types of yoga schools, there are also several meditation practices to choose from. I follow transcendental meditation, and these are the basic rules to get you started.

Find a quiet place to sit in silence for fifteen or twenty minutes daily. It's best to meditate in the morning when you get up and later on during the mid-afternoon. Sit on the floor with your back straight and legs crossed. (Or in a chair with your feet touching the ground.) Rest your hands on your lap, join the tips of your thumb and index fingers together to form a full circle. Close your eyes and focus your attention on your breathing. Breathe in and breathe out through your nose. Internally repeat "oh" when inhaling and "mmm" when exhaling. Though your mind will probably stray and wander, this is normal. Thoughts rush in trying to distract you from your breathing. Without getting angry or impatient, bring your attention back to your inhalations and exhalations.

The purpose of meditation is not to think about anything. Contrary to what many believe, sitting down to meditate does not mean to think deeply about a subject, but to clear your mind and experience emptiness. That same emptiness creates order and trains you in the skill of controlling your thoughts instead of being controlled by them. Be aware that perfecting the art of meditation takes years, but its benefits are huge. Studies conducted on people who meditate show that it improves health and even lengthens life.

♠ ♠ ♠ ♠ ♥

As you can see, there are several disciplines and resources available that can help you find the necessary emotional, spiritual, and psychological calmness to envision and accomplish your professional goals. Keep in mind that it's not easy to find the success you're looking for alone or with your family's support. You'll soon find the need to extend your contact network in order to explore tools you haven't used thus far. Most importantly, I wouldn't want you to abandon your dreams just because you find them hard to attain.

Chapter 2

What Messages Did You Receive and What Messages Do You Send Out Without Knowing?

Famous Women Speak: Cristina Saralegui

This Cuban-born journalist needs no introduction. The host of Univision's "El Show de Cristina" for twenty-one years and winner of twelve Emmys, she's one of the most famous and influential figures in U.S. Hispanic entertainment. In 1999 she became the first Spanish-language television celebrity to receive a star on the Hollywood Walk of Fame. A successful businesswoman to boot, in 2004 she launched Casa Cristina, a line of furniture and decorative items sold in Sears and Kmart stores throughout the U.S.

Q: *What did your parents dream for you and what were your dreams as a child?*

A: Ever since I can remember I was surrounded by books. I've spent most of my life reading. I think this goes hand in hand with the fact that I'm a curious person, and I'm very interested in knowing how things work. When I was a child I thought I'd become a writer. When I started studying at the University of Miami, my dad advised me to take up journalism because, the way he saw it, a degree in journalism would afford me more opportunities to get a job; he knew many writers who couldn't make ends meet. In hindsight, I think that was a wise piece of advice.

Q: *Why did you decide to move from print media to television? How did you make it happen?*

A: During the last year of my journalism studies I did an internship at *Vanidades* magazine. In my native Cuba, *Vanidades* had been part of my family's investment portfolio; that's how my dad was able to get me the internship and how I started off in the magazine world. I was fascinated with it, though I had a hard time adapting since I had always studied in English and didn't quite manage Spanish. With the help of an English/Spanish dictionary I learned enough vocabulary to communicate well. I enjoyed this experience so much that I stayed with the publishing company for over twenty years. I went from editing to directing several magazines until I became the director of *Cosmopolitan's* Spanish edition. While I was serving as director of *Cosmo en Español,* I was invited by Don Francisco (Mario Kreutzberger) to participate on a panel dealing with women's issues on his program "Sábado Gigante." This was around 1988. I did so well that Don Francisco invited me to join him for ten additional programs. At the end of this cycle, Don Francisco recommended me to the president of the broadcasting company, Mr. Joaquin Blaya, for a project he had in mind, a talk show similar to Oprah Winfrey's. That's how I had the chance to move from print media to television.

Q: *Which are your fondest memories as host of "El Show de Cristina?"*

A: I've interviewed many celebrities and I've always enjoyed those interviews as I have a great relationship with the majority of the celebrities given my long trajectory in the media. But I've always relished those heroes no one knows about and whom I had the privilege of meeting on my show. Such was the case with a program we did right after the

9/11 Twin Towers tragedy in New York; walking through the rubble and destruction; shaking hands, embracing or speaking words of encouragement to the Hispanic policemen and firefighters performing challenging rescue tasks; that touched my soul deeply. Some experiences leave an imprint that could last a lifetime. This was one of them. On a lighter note, some guests are unforgettable. Like the young Dominican man who called himself "The Lover," an incorrigible womanizer who always made us laugh with his comments and witty remarks. So much so that even today The Lover still pops up in conversations with my producers. There have been lots of characters like him.

Q: *Of all your professional achievements so far, which have been the most rewarding and why?*

A: All professional achievements throughout a lengthy career are rewarding since one gives rise to the next. But one that was extremely rewarding was the time I was awarded the star on the Hollywood Walk of Fame. It was the first star awarded to a Hispanic television celebrity. I really loved it because I thought I had once again overcome the barrier, and that this would earmark the courage Hispanic people living in the States have; we cannot be marginalized. The greatest satisfaction was seeing how many people stood by me that day. I remember that there was such a huge turnout, they had to block access to Hollywood Boulevard. Though this created a sizeable chaos, it clearly displayed the power of the masses and of our people in this country. It moved me so much I bought a full page ad in Los Angeles' *La Opinión* newspaper to thank all those people who took time from their busy schedules, and even took off from work to be with me and support me that day. I'd like to thank them once again for such show of affection.

Q: *What does success mean to you?*

A: Having creative control over my projects.

Q: *What keeps you motivated to continue growing in your career?*
A: It's not so much growing in my career, but a matter of feeding my vocational needs as a communicator.

Blanca Rosa Vilchez, the national correspondent from New York on "Noticiero Univision," was brought up in Peru with four brothers and a younger sister. And though in many Hispanic homes this would be the perfect setting for a female to take care of all the men's needs, Blanca Rosa was lucky to have a liberal father. Instead of expecting less from her he was even more demanding than with her brothers. "My father used to say things like, education is important for everyone but even more so for women because if their marriage fails, they have to make sure they're independent and not remain with their husbands for financial reasons," says the news reporter who's been at Univision since 1987.

Unfortunately, this is not the case for a great number of women who, regardless of their age or native country, have consciously or subconsciously received messages that contributed to defining roles, expectations, and responsibilities set for them. For example, Martha Alicia Chávez Martínez, a famous Mexican writer and psychotherapist says, "Changes have taken place over time; when I was a little girl and a teenager, my culture did not encourage females to better themselves or achieve great goals, etc. Today, there's greater acceptance and open-mindedness about women doing things beyond the walls of their homes and beyond the roles conventionally expected of them."

How was it in your case? Head down memory lane and try to remember. What games did you play? I don't mean it in the sense that girls play with dolls and boys play with cars. This corresponds to the biological differences detected in scientific studies where the male brain tends to summarize, i.e., organize systems and discover how things work, so that they sometimes have a greater affinity for objects than for people. Females, on the other hand, tend to establish empathy with others, study their tone of voice, needs, feelings, etc., thus their greater affinity for individuals.[1] On the contrary, I'm referring to the fact that, in addition to one's biological predisposition, there's a tendency among parents to encourage women to cooperate with others at playtime (playing doctor, teacher, and mom), while men are encouraged to compete (battleship, videogames, car racing). Girls must be good and boys must be strong; girls may overtly express their feelings and boys should hide them ("boys don't cry"), and this approach to parenting is conveyed in different ways during one's childhood.

How does this transmission take place? A thousand different ways. It may be how parents react to the same story told by a boy or a girl; the boy is cheered on for having hit a classmate who stole his toy and the girl is scolded for having done the exact same thing. Boys are often encouraged to get up and keep playing after being kicked by a playmate during soccer practice; girls are pampered and asked to sit down for a while until the pain subsides.

Now think, what household chores did you have at home? What were your responsibilities? Mine included setting and picking up the table, washing dishes on weekends, serving the food, and watering the plants. My brother never had to deal with that. He might have had to wash my dad's car, and I think I remember he even got paid for it. Perhaps what was expected from you and your brothers in terms of household chores was different in your case or not so clear cut. But even today, and in spite of the greater number of men helping out, women tend to be the ones responsi-

1. *The Essential Difference: Male and Female Brains and the Truth About Autism*, Simon Baron-Cohen. Basic Books, 2003.

ble for running the house smoothly.[2] And, to top it off, today's women work as hard as men!

Try to remember, what extracurricular activities were you involved in? I took dancing, ceramics, English classes, and piano lessons. I was never encouraged to watch or practice competitive sports. Though, if I had been, it might have helped me trust in my physical strength some more, and, subsequently, improve my self-esteem. Nor did I participate in math or science competitions, or in events geared toward sparking possible career interests. Things were different for my brother when he was a kid. My father not only took him to soccer games, but to his surgical procedures dressed as miniature doctor from a very young age.

YOUR VOICE THROUGH SOCIAL NETWORKS

"*Money is not important, intelligence and culture are; love for the arts is more significant than love for money; prestige is more important than success.* Though I thank my parents for conveying their love for knowledge and wisdom through these mandates, as an adult I had to face the fact that in a world ruled by material things, money and success played an important role when becoming competent and fighting for my individual development. My parents, an intellectual and cultural couple, raised me on the idea that it was better to have a higher cultural level than a socioeconomic one. When you grow up you realize that if you want to truly advance in your career, you must have a little bit of everything."
—*Gilberta Caron, Argentine writer and songwriter for Walt Disney and Universal Music, via Facebook*

In the U.S. it's not only common for girls and boys to attend all sorts of sports events, but to also participate in competitive sports:

2. *Successful Professional Women of the Americas*, Betty Jane Punnett et al. Edward Elgar Publishing Ltd., 2006.

soccer, baseball, basketball, and more. In addition, schools and NGOs offer a broad selection of clubs, camps, and competitions in fields like engineering, science, math, finance, business development, etc., for females and males alike. But in regions like Latin America these options seldom include women. (And I suggest if you're living in the U.S., and have daughters living here too, reconsider some of your own biases picked up during your upbringing in your native country.)

This quick tour of some of the possible subliminal messages we may have received as children will help you to bear them in mind and "deconstruct" them when your inner voice tries to throw sand in the gears. It's best to learn how to disidentify with them. And hopefully, it will also remind you that you're constantly externalizing verbal and nonverbal messages about who you are, what you want to achieve, and how much you trust you'll accomplish what you set out to do. If the messages you send to the universe and to your professional environment are aligned with your goals, they'll be more easily attainable. Otherwise, the journey will be tougher.

THE VOICE OF EXPERIENCE

"I wouldn't change a thing of what I was told during my childhood. Everything I was told and what was done to me in the past is part of who I am today. Though there may have been some negative things like "you can't do this," those words only made me stronger and gave me enough strength to change *you can't* into *oh, yes I can.*"
—Carla Dodds, Senior Director, Marketing Retail Formats for Walmart Brazil

---

If you really want to be successful, you must have a clear idea what your goals are. I suggest you take a thorough look at the inventory of possible childhood messages I offer in this chapter (which will undoubtedly trigger others), and identify which ones are still lingering. The goal is to split that old message into small units and pick out any negative connotations that might still affect you today. Only then will you be able to create a new and clear message for yourself and a world that better matches what you're after.

How Do the Messages and Mandates We Receive Work?

When I was a child, my father always used to say I was clumsy. I guess some of my actions must have inspired his theory, but he also had his own way of conditioning my behavior so I could confirm his theory and prove he was right. For instance, every time he saw me walking with a tray piled with dishes and glasses he'd say, "Be careful not to drop it." I didn't do it on purpose, but eight out of ten times I would drop the tray confirming once again that I was always "the clumsy" one. I suppose, subconsciously, it was my way of getting his attention, of fitting into the idea he had about me in order not to lose his love. I was convinced that I was clumsy until I got married at twenty-four. My husband never paid attention to that detail and I eventually stopped breaking dishes as often. I realized there was nothing clumsy about me; it was just the memory of a silly word I had believed to be true.

Some Examples to Trigger Your Memories

It's impossible to build an inventory of all the messages you've received either directly or indirectly over time. A lot will depend on your age, the country you grew up in, your parents' or grandparents' mindset, your social class, and even your religion. This humble inventory of negative messages (though I'm sure you've also received lots of positive ones!) is intended to help you review whether the personal beliefs you so strongly hold on to about yourself are opinions or ideas that others have about you that need to be set aside today. To continue believing in them only limits your growth possibilities. These messages usually attack various aspects of your womanhood.

1) Verbal messages

> Children should be seen and not heard.
> Doing this or that is not ladylike (climbing, swings, getting dirty, fighting, etc.).
> Don't be a tomboy (or equivalents).
> Let's leave the men to talk while we go to the kitchen and get the coffee ready.
> It's important to marry someone who's well-off.
> The main thing is for you to get married and have children.
> When a little boy cries: "Come on, boys don't cry." When a little girl cries: "What's the matter, honey?"
> When a boy tries to perform a physical feat: "You can do it! Don't be afraid!" When a girl attempts it: "Careful, you may get hurt!"
> Wow, you're smart (or any other adjective) *for a girl*.
> "[Those] comments made explaining why a woman was in a high-level position, *She probably slept with . . .*", says Mariel Fiori, Director of the New Jersey–based magazine *Tu Voz*, regarding the prevalence of men in the journalism world in her motherland of Argentina.
> *That* (whatever activity) is not for women.
> "What I'd like to change is what I was told as a kid, 'What's there to do?' This sentence implies that you give up before starting the battle. That we have no control over what's happening, and that we're all victims of destiny. I don't think so! This sentence is like psychological

poison that undermines the way in which we make decisions. It makes us not want to try our best to achieve our goals," says Anna Giraldo-Kerr, Founder and President of Shades for Success Coaching Inc.

➤ You can't do *that* because you're a woman.

➤ "How could you let your sister stick up for you?" My father asked my brother after I hit a girl back who, in turn, had hit my brother but he didn't want to retaliate because she was a girl," shares Leylha Ahuile, the founder of the online magazine *Tinta Fresca*, via Twitter.

➤ You must dress prim and proper.

➤ Don't speak until spoken to.

➤ Are you a virgin? (Though men weren't expected to be, it was assumed that women had to remain virgins until their wedding night.)

➤ "If you look at yourself naked in the mirror, you'll see the image of the devil." (What nuns used to tell the writer Martha Alicia Chávez Martínez.)

➤ "I always had small breasts and when I was a teenager, one of my aunts used to tell me that if she had enough money, she would give it to me so I could fix my boobs. Others would ask me if I'd considered plastic surgery. I think there's this conception that Latinas should have big breasts, and if you happen to have small ones, you are considered something less than a woman," reveals Jazmin Cameron, Communications Director of Latinos incollege.com.

➤ Wealthy people aren't happy.

➤ I don't understand why she's always concerned about work and neglects her family.

2) Nonverbal messages

> Men sit at the head of the table and must always be served first.
> Men (dad, uncle, brother) come home and switch the television channel that you or other women were watching without even asking permission.
> Men drive when riding with a woman on board.
> Men handle the big bucks and women the petty cash.
> Men are in charge of big negotiation deals: buying a car, a house, etc.

YOUR VOICE THROUGH SOCIAL NETWORKS

"I remember the time I broke up with the boyfriend I was living with and went back to my parents' home. My brothers were still in high school and lived at home. One evening, my dad came back home and yelled at me for not picking up my brothers' mess. I thought it was stupid of him to expect me to act as a sleep-in housekeeper. It was definitely a sexist comment on his part."

—*Diane Librizzi, CEO and Executive Producer of La Loca Entertainment, via Facebook*

> Men can (and often do!) have lovers, and this is accepted as a de facto standard; women can't.
> In Latin America women carry their father's last name until they get married and add the possessive "*de*" after their first and last name. For example: Juana Salcedo de Díaz. In the U.S., women abandon their maiden name and adopt their husband's. Therefore, they never *really* have a name of their own.

> At social gatherings, men in your family are asked about their jobs/careers and you are asked about your social or family activities.

> "My brothers were allowed to have girlfriends and I wasn't. I'm twenty-one years old and my mom still doesn't like me to go out with men," says Vikki Campos, student at Barnard College, via Facebook.

> Girls are encouraged to play more structured games where they follow rules imposed by adults, while boys take part in more unstructured activities where they can enforce their own rules, lead, and be more aggressive.

> In terms of household chores, the majority of yours were considered your family contribution and you had to fulfill them regularly. Your brothers had more infrequent chores like cleaning the tool room or mowing the lawn, and were often paid for doing so. Also, chores typically assigned to women require certain monitoring while those assigned to men encourage their independence.

> You attended a Catholic school (or one or both parents were very religious) where you were forced to confess more often than men in your family, and attention was placed in making you feel guilty, disgraceful, and weak for actions that were excused in men.

> In your environment there was this notion that women always needed to be rescued, not only in the movies and in children's book, but in politics, business, and at home. Persistent stereotypes exist where men are still almost always heroes and women poor weaklings that must be rescued. (*Snow White*, *Sleeping Beauty* and more recently, *Toy Story*.)

> "If I wanted to do something, my parents assumed I

could do it on my own even if I desperately sought their help. Yet they held my brother's hand and helped him through all his battles," says Melissa Bee via Facebook.

The truth is, these habits and expressions are so ingrained in many of our cultures that the work to be done not only entails detaching from old childhood mandates but also being watchful about what you take in daily. And if you have daughters, this exercise will help you be aware of the messages you send to them consciously and unconsciously.

THE VOICE OF EXPERIENCE

"Some years back, I was offered an opportunity to give a series of courses to a powerful company in northern Mexico. It entailed staying for a week in that city. Of course I said yes. Two or three days later the project director called me up to say that I wouldn't be doing the job and that they were hiring a man. I was 100% qualified to deliver the course and I asked why they changed their minds. Answers were evasive and ridiculous. I exerted a lot pressure with my questions demanding a justified reason for my removal from the project. He ultimately admitted that his wife was jealous about me going to the city and staying at the same hotel where he'd be for a week. I was very annoyed. I went to speak to his wife to tell her there was no reason for her to be concerned, that I was very professional and didn't fool around with married men. I gave her my word that nothing was going to happen with her husband, and I told her I needed that project. She answered, "Oh, Martha, the point is you're divorced." And added that it was him she mistrusted. I tried to make her understand that in order for something to happen between us I would have to agree and that wasn't my plan. I repeated the same idea in different ways, my promise, commitment, oath, that I was uninterested in her husband. She wasn't supportive. And, believe it or not, I was left out of the picture, for a simple and ridiculous act of jealousy by the director's wife. Of course I didn't walk out of his office before telling him some truths about his lack of manhood."

—*Martha Alicia Chávez Martínez, Mexican writer and psychologist*

The Social Environment You Were Raised In

I don't want to avoid touching on a subject that is seldom mentioned yet impacts opportunities each of us has access to, and our ability to know how to tap into them when they come up. The socioeconomic and educational setting you grew up in has a powerful influence throughout the different phases of your life. If your parents had a limited education and you grew up in a humble environment, it's likely that you didn't have access to private schools, tutors or special programs in your childhood.

If such was the case, it's also likely that you didn't have a chance to be exposed to another set of elements which, over time, you'll have to somehow offset. Elements such as conversations about influential people and deep analysis of political, economic, historical or current events; discussions about art, music, culture; international travels (to destinations outside of your native country); appropriate manners to socialize with top-notch professionals and stakeholder groups; memberships to influential institutions, and most importantly, access to social circles that open doors throughout your career.

THE VOICE OF EXPERIENCE

"Because I am a Latina who grew up in the Dominican Republic, I tend to see things from a broad perspective informed by my gender, ethnicity, and global lens. To me, the biggest obstacles to creating an inclusive and thriving workplace are the subtle or unconscious biases which are part of the human condition. At one time or another, it is likely that we have all been both the perpetrators and targets and more often than not, we aren't really aware of it. Whether they are positive or negative—as in the hardworking immigrant or the sexy Latina—whether they are manifested in preferential or overtly dismissive forms, as in special allowances for someone who is nice but who would benefit from receiving frank feedback or not hiring someone because 'they're not the right fit,' they limit our ability to see a person accurately and can often marginalize individuals. In the workplace, this is often reflected in terms of underutilized people and untapped potential. With the best of intentions, we include or exclude people based on the categories or groups to which they belong, not on their potential or abilities as individuals. I believe that until we make a concerted effort to recognize the biases in others and ourselves and thoughtfully address them, individuals from traditionally marginalized groups will continue to face obstacles in the workplace."

—*Daisy Auger-Domínguez, VP, Organizational and Workforce Diversity at Disney ABC Television Group*

Here's a situation I come upon daily. One of my best friends, Susan, is Anglo-Saxon and lives in an upper middle class neighborhood in New York. Her fourteen-year-old daughter, Abby, can recite Russia's history since World War II to date for ten solid minutes straight. She can debate with her parents on contemporary politics, classical music, the best chefs in the country, and hundreds of other subjects she's exposed to daily, not just in school but through interactions with her family and their friends.

At the dinner table, Abby and her ten-year-old sister, Emma, talk with their parents about: what happened at school, news articles from *The New York Times*, conflicts at their parents' workplaces, IBM's weekend program (Emma was chosen for it) and how they learned to freeze a flower or pierce a balloon with a pin without bursting it, how to improve Abby's timing for a swim meet that weekend by one thousandth of a second, and how to get Home Depot to lend a scaffold to the Girl Scout group that Susan leads so they can paint a school mural for children with special needs.

Thanks to these types of conversations and exposure to various experiences, Abby and Emma know how to behave at a five star restaurant, how to talk about interesting subjects with adults, how to write a report, how to lead a school team, and thousands of other subtle skills that subconsciously prepare them to be successful at college and later on in their careers.

This is not the case with the majority of Hispanic students who are often the first in their families to attend college. These young-sters (and your situation may be similar) didn't enjoy this type of exchange with their parents. Many had to work during their high school years; many had to figure out alone what steps to follow to go on to college. Many enrolled in a two-year college program or technical school because they believed it was their only option. And even when they were admitted to excellent colleges many found it hard to adapt to that college culture where the majority of students knew about the nonverbal social rules and had what is known as the cultural capital the majority of Hispanic students lacked.

Over time, that social and cultural gap may interfere with your professional growth and the only way to overcome it is by ac-knowledging it's there and seeking help. That help can take many forms, from mentors and advisers to private coaches, self-help books, and specialized courses. Sometimes you think your prob-lem is your accent when, ultimately, the problem is that you don't know how to express your thoughts or don't have the level of ver-bal subtlety for third parties to take you seriously. Perhaps you're not familiar with the cultural references used at the workplace; or don't understand the codes everyone understands without needing an explanation.

THE VOICE OF EXPERIENCE

"I was lucky that my parents liked opera, classical music, going to Broadway shows and crazy pictures. That really helped me because you must be able to talk about a variety of subjects. Talking about things other than work plays a significant role in developing your contact network. It's easier for men because they play golf or go to clubs where they smoke cigars, make conversation, and get to know each other. Things are tougher for women because there's so much we've got to do: be educated, get married, raise a family, work . . . but you've got to try and find 'that extra something' that makes you interesting and allows you to expand on. I once spoke to someone who was just starting her career and said her company had organized an outing to a Broadway show. Since she had never been to one, she decided not to go with the group because she didn't know the dress code. You can't let that stop you! You've got to find someone who's been to a show and ask the dumbest questions you can think of: when should I clap, what should I wear . . . ? But you mustn't limit yourself just because you've never been exposed to that type of event. It's in situations like these that you can get to talk to others and share a bit more of your personal story."

—*Catherine McKenzie, Senior Producer of ABC's*
"Good Morning America"

Much of what's in these pages is geared toward identifying those socioeconomic, cultural, or educational gaps, and present to you ways to overcome them. If you aren't aware that the manner in which you express yourself and solve conflicts is not only connected to your culture and gender but also to the social environment you grew up in, you'll find it hard to act accordingly and fill those gaps.

There's nothing more effective in bringing about change than identifying the difficulty (something which is discomforting enough to want to abandon), and seeking a better option. But the truth is, we only detach ourselves from these limitations when we've truly grown uncomfortable with them. And if you don't believe me, think about how many times you've heard your friend complain about her job and repeatedly say she wants to quit. Why doesn't she do it already? Because she still doesn't feel uncomfortable enough with the situation to warrant the risk entailed in quitting and looking for another job.

♥   ♥   ♥   ♥   ♥

EXERCISE: Rewrite Your Messages

Tap into this moment where I've refreshed your memory to make your own list of memorable or subliminal messages you received during your childhood and teenage years.

- Write down the message. For example: "Stop talking like that, you sound like a man."
- Break down the sentence so you can understand it better. In this case, if I speak with confidence, showing self-assurance, or let people know when there's something I don't like, I'm no longer that good, nice, and exemplary girl I was brought up to be.
- Internally forgive your parents (or whoever said such things) because they did their best, with the tools and knowledge they had, and, in the majority of cases, without ill intention.
- Reconsider what truth there is in this message; do you really believe you'll stop being a woman by expressing your opinions or showing confidence in yourself?
- Recognize there's nothing useful about that old broken record at this stage in your life and replace it with a message that aligns with your goals. For example, "It's important to express myself clearly and concisely so that my ideas have a strong impact."

Once you've completed your list of messages, you'll have fresh inventory that's more in tune with your present situation.

♠   ♠   ♠   ♠   ♠

Chapter 3

The Creative Power of Language

Famous Women Speak: Soledad O'Brien

Soledad O'Brien is a widely recognized broadcast journalist and anchor of the CNN morning show "Starting Point." After coanchoring "American Morning" (where she covered the aftermath of Hurricane Katrina) for four years, Soledad went on to become the anchor for several CNN special documentary series such as "Black in America," "Latino in America," and "Gay in America." I've seen Soledad, the daughter of a black Cuban mother and a white Australian father, present keynote speeches numerous times. She is one of the few multiracial journalists at the forefront of the industry and she takes this responsibility seriously. Regardless of whether she's speaking in front of a large audience, one-on-one, or interviewing a tough subject for her show, Soledad is always engaging, down-to-earth and warm. This is her signature style.

Q: *As a journalist, language is a key tool for you. How have you used language for career growth?*

A: Language is one of the most critical things a journalist learns early on. You have to be able to turn a story you hear into a story fit for TV. You also have to learn to take a great idea that's in your head and articulate it to your boss. So, I've learned to harness language for my job. In my professional life, I work hard at saying no. I have lots of interests, and I like doing things for people. I also realize I'm the face of African Latinas. So I have a tough time turning people down. I'm almost forty-six years old, and I only now feel I got good at saying no. I also feel I got better at telling my story and at how I want to be perceived. I got better at negotiating with my bosses, at asking for the stories I want to cover like Haiti and the tsunami.

Q: *What are some of the strategies that have worked best for you as a multiracial woman when it comes to career advancement?*

A: Two things. One, I have a great sense of humor when it comes to what people are freaking out about. For example, as a mother, when people were concerned about sending me out to cover stories like the tsunami, and they'd say, "You're a mom, you're not going to want to go." I'd laugh and reply, 'I am a mom, and with four kids under the age of four, an eighteen-hour plane ride seems like a good idea—send me! I'm dying to go.' People understood that I wanted to go. Not in a strident and demanding way, which is not my style, but in *jokey* way, 'who more than me wants to get on a plane?' It allowed people to realize that what they had said may have been inappropriate, or that they had misunderstood me, while keeping it light. I think it helped change their minds rather than creating a confrontation. Two, I'm very clear. This is what I want to say, this is what I can do, this is where I want to go. And I've been very good at not sharing personal issues. My bosses don't need to know what I'm worried about, they don't need to know that my babysitter went on vacation. All they need to know is that I will be there and I will make it happen. People in general share too much and bosses don't really want to deal with your problems. They want the job done. I get it. My job is to show them that I'm a good employee under any circumstances.

Q: *Coming from a family where six out of six siblings went to Harvard, there must*

42

have been some serious mandates at home both spoken and unspoken. Can you think of a few of them?

A: The only mandate they articulated was their obsession for us to be kind people. We had to treat each other well, we had to be our own best friends because there weren't a lot of people who looked like us. We were not allowed to pick on each other. We were very close.

Q: *When your siblings had gone to Harvard, did you feel pressure to follow in their footsteps?*

A: I knew if my sister got in, I could get in because I was as smart as she was, but my parents never pushed us to go to Harvard. Not in a million years would they do that. They just said, "You should go where you are happy." I felt the genuine pressure of being around smart people. You had to come with a good argument if you wanted to have a conversation with them. My siblings are smart people.

Q: *You have four kids of your own. Two daughters, twelve and ten, and eight-year-old twin sons. Do you feel that moms unconsciously tend to raise girls with slightly different messages than boys?*

A: No, I think that's changing a little bit, actually for me. It depends more on the kid. I have some kids who are more athletic and when they get hurt they need to be told "go, go, go, jump back in," and others who need more consoling. My parents were definitely stricter with the girls than they were with the boys.

Q: *What is success for you?*

A: I think success for me is checking a lot of different boxes. There's an element of professional success and an element of personal success, like success in your family. Are you a happy and accomplished person? Things like, can I hold a pose in yoga, can I make my horse jump over that fence, can I run five miles. Am I intellectually able to achieve things

I really want to achieve? Am I turning out work I am proud of? Am I a good mom, do I learn from my mistakes? Are my children respectful, are they kind to other people? The values my parents had, I have as well.

Q: *Do you consider yourself successful?*

A: Yes, I do. I had enough professional success and I'm happy. I look at my work and I look at my kids and I say I do a good job. My definition of success is not just my title. Success has to be a measure of impact on others. So far so good, I feel pretty good of my forty-five years on the planet.

Before moving on I'd like to explore the creative power of language. In the first chapter I asked you to examine your reality in language (e.g., "I'm paralyzed"). Let's take a deeper look at how this notion works and how you can benefit from it to shake off those old messages and create a new reality more in tune with your imagination and aspirations.

Just like a fish in water unaware of its environment because it's all its ever known, us humans live submerged in language. Unaware that is, until someone takes it out of water or its natural environment. Language humanizes us; that's why human beings who have been abandoned in the wilderness without contact with other humans and who haven't learned how to communicate with words wind up assimilating to animals they live with.[1]

Language (spoken, nonverbal, thoughts and gestures) permeates all our experiences. Consider this for a moment, without language you couldn't read these words, or assess what you're reading, or you couldn't believe in God because you wouldn't have the words to explain that belief or concept of a higher being. It's impossible to detach yourself from language except during deep

1. *L'Enigme des enfants-loups*, Serge Aroles. Editions Publibook, 2007.

meditation, given that its precise purpose is to silence the constant flow pouring from our brain.

THE VOICE OF EXPERIENCE

"The way we express ourselves generates a myriad of ideas about ourselves in others, about our clothing, hair style, etc. It's a way of showing yourself."

—*Lina Meruane, Literature Professor at New York University*

Language plays numerous roles. Today I'd like you to observe the way you use it in everyday life and the impact it has on you and others. Let's start with an example: Alice is a ten-year-old girl. Her mother gave her $5.00 and sent her to the grocer's alone for the very first time to buy milk that cost $1.50. On her way home, Alice saw a girl her age asking for alms and gave her $1.00. When she returned home she gave her mom the milk and $2.50 change. Her mom said, "Congratulations on going to the store all by yourself, Alice!" And when she counted the money she added, "But sweetie, they gave you back the wrong change. You're just like your father, you'll never learn math!" Alice felt so badly she didn't tell her mom what she had done with the missing dollar.

The following week, her mother needed something from the supermarket and asked Alice's older brother in the presence of Alice, "John, please go to the supermarket and buy coffee and sugar," and John, who was watching television, replied, "Why don't you send Alice?" His mother answered, "No, you go. She's not good at math and brings back the wrong change." A week later, Alice got a low grade on her math test. When she showed it to her mother, her mom remarked, "Well, we already know you're not good at math, right? What is important is that you're doing well in reading."

During subsequent weeks and months, several events took

place that reinforced the idea that Alice was not good in math. For instance, although her school could enroll students to participate in the state's math competition, her mother didn't encourage her to join as did several of her classmates' mothers. Alice grew frustrated and instead of studying harder to achieve better grades in math, she thought, *why should I study if I'll do poorly anyway?* The less she prepared, the worse grades she received, and this vicious cycle wound up restricting her from taking advanced math courses in high school. Years later, it would limit her opportunities for admission to certain prestigious colleges.

Of course, this is an oversimplified example of the kind of exchanges that happen in homes all the time. We don't realize the impact words have in shaping the future of a person. Alice trusts her mom's words most in this world, but little did Alice's mom know how much her words affected her daughter. (For some other girl with a different personality, these words could have had the opposite effect, giving her the necessary strength to show her mother she was wrong and that she could excel in math and in whatever she set her mind to.)

For Alice, who grew up hearing that she resembled her dad in many positive ways as well, her mother's words were real, and so she began to act accordingly. There came a point where everybody started to believe that her problem was innate, i.e., everybody ended up believing "she was always bad at math." (Mind you, I'm not suggesting there aren't kids with greater skills than others in specific areas, I'm saying that, given the same skill sets and different language use, some children will have greater chances to succeed than others.) That's why it's so important to be aware of the great power of language to generate all kinds of realities.

Let's examine the situation. Out of everything I told you, the only observable "fact" (i.e., "measurable" fact) is that Alice went to the market and brought back $2.50 change. Her mother's statement, "You're just like your father, you'll never learn math!" is simply her own interpretation of what happened. In this case, as we know, the truth was otherwise unknown to her mother.

Let's look at Alice twenty-five years from now, as a thirty-five-year-old adult whose boss tells her she should take some finance courses so she could be promoted to department manager. Alice takes her first lesson, flunks the exam, and abandons the course. Her explanation (or excuse) is that she was never good with numbers. The truth is that this idea stemmed from her mother's *interpretation* of a fact that she (the mother) had gotten wrong to start with. But Alice's own beliefs and self-perception regarding that incident had a bearing on how she listened to her mother's interpretation, leading her to believe in it and act accordingly.

So now the question is: Does it do Alice any good to continue thinking she's bad at math? This belief will impact her actions which, in turn, will influence career results obtained. Ultimately, it's time Alice realized it no longer matters whether her mother was right or wrong. What matters is that Alice should understand that her mother's interpretation about her, which she believed and sustained for so many years, is no longer useful for achieving the results she's looking for. She must therefore abandon that belief and create a new interpretation to replace it.

♥   ♥   ♥   ♥   ♥

How to Transform Facts into Words and Words into Results

It's good to always be aware of this sequence: 1) facts become words; 2) words become beliefs; 3) and these become actions that lead to certain results. I will help you identify how language influences results obtained and those you failed to obtain in life.

- An observable event or experience takes place. (Alice brought back $2.50 in change; $1.00 less than the difference between the $5.00 her mom gave her and the price of milk $1.50.)

- You select certain data and details about what you observe. (Alice heard her mother scolding her because she brought back the wrong change. She didn't listen to her mother commending her on her independence. She also didn't explain to her mother what happened with the change, which would have corrected the misconception regarding the math.)

- You add meaning to your observations by including personal and cultural elements. (Alice's mother believes people are born being good or bad at math, and Alice grew up totally convinced that her mother was right. For being "just like her dad," who isn't swift with numbers, she probably must be so, too. Nobody is taking into account the fact that her father never finished elementary school, and he's therefore not likely to understand much about math.)

- You build assumptions based on the meaning assigned to events, and draw conclusions you believe represent "the truth." (Alice's mother assumed her daughter was bad at math and just like her father because she brought back the wrong change. That became the truth for the mother, then for Alice, and later on for Alice's brother. In truth, this statement was just the mother's assumption based on data she chose from reality, and in this case the data was wrong.)

- You adopt beliefs related to the world around you. (Alice thought there was no chance she'd do well on her school test, and later on at work because her experience showed she was not good with numbers.)

- You start acting based on your beliefs. (Alice stopped studying and started receiving bad grades which reinforced her belief about her poor math skills; and the vicious cycle was thus created. Once that belief was established, she dragged it on for the rest of her life because it became part of her reality. When her boss told her to take a course in finance, that old broken record started playing again in her head and she became paralyzed.)

Once you reach the action phase, you're pretty far removed from the event itself. Reviewing these steps may help you deconstruct obsolete messages. It's easy to do when you acknowledge it all starts when you choose certain data over the other in any given event. Always remember that the event and the explanation of the event—which you infuse with your own experience, feelings, etc.—are two different things.[2]

♠   ♠   ♠   ♠   ♠

The Value of Distinctions

It may help to think as follows: each one of us observes the world through a set of *distinctions*. According to language ontology, a discipline whose leading representatives are Humberto Maturana, Fernando Flores, Rafael Echeverría, and Julio Olalla,[3] distinctions

---

2. Outline based on *Language and the Pursuit of Happiness*, Chalmers Brothers. New Possibilities Press, 2005.
3. *Del ser al hacer*, Humberto Maturana. Granica, 2009.
   El observador y su mundo, Rafael Echeverría. Garnica, 2009.
   Ontología del lenguaje, Rafael Echeverría. Granica, 2000.
   From Knowledge to Wisdom, Julio Olalla. Newfield Network Inc., 2004.

are concepts, ideas or terms through which we see the world. They're not mere definitions of objects or concepts; rather they enable us to see what we wouldn't see without them. For example, a person studying in the U.S. knows what SAT, ACT, GPA, AP, and IB mean, and also knows how these may influence your college admission and success. If you don't have these distinctions, you can hardly act on them, i.e., you won't prepare or sit for the SAT/ACT exams on time, you won't take advanced AP or IB courses, and you won't be concerned about keeping up your grade point average during high school.

These distinctions reside within language. Perhaps not until someone had told you that the SAT was critical to college entry had you even acknowledged the exam back when you were a teenager. Something similar happened to me recently. I had never heard about a much acclaimed speaker (according to the person who introduced me to him), but the day after I met him, I noticed this man was presenting at several of the same conferences I was. What happened? Was it suddenly by chance that we were together everywhere? No. We were at the same conferences before, too, (as I was able to confirm after reviewing programs) but I didn't know him, I didn't "distinguish" him among the long list of speakers.

THE VOICE OF EXPERIENCE

"Some time ago, my professional coach said to me, 'your career is a marathon; you have to take it as a journey so that you don't get overly stressed by daily occurrences.' It immediately dawned on me that in Spanish *carrera* can mean both a professional career and a speed race (car race: *carrera de auto*) or running race. That makes us feel competitive and stressed; we're just not able to relax. To reach that place where you don't feel you're running a race, you must think of your professional life as being on a path."

—*Ruth Gaviria, Senior Vice President Corporate Marketing for Univision*

Sometimes, the only thing you need to further your career is to generate new distinctions in certain areas. For instance, by asking a mentor to clarify your company's unwritten rules you can discover options you didn't even know existed. Or if your communication style clashes with your company's culture, you may need to ask your mentor to give you specific feedback on how to improve your style. Or, if you own a business, somebody should clearly explain what benefits you may reap if you certify your company as a Minority-Owned Business or a Woman-Owned Business in order to obtain agreements with large companies or government contracts.

If nobody points these things out to you, how will you acquire the distinctions needed to decide whether you want to make a change or not? Without this knowledge, you'll continue finding nonproductive explanations to your unsatisfactory results.

THE VOICE OF EXPERIENCE

Speaking of the power of language, Lina Meruane, a Chilean writer and literature professor at New York University remarks, "The hardest thing in this regard is to go into a language you don't fully master. I recently understood that I sounded rude in English, maybe even aggressive, with people who were interviewing me for a job because I didn't handle the super-delicate code they did. It was a job interview over the phone and, unfortunately, the interviewers got the worst impression. One of the questions was about a subject that had absolutely nothing to do with the job I was applying for. I got very nervous and asked them to rephrase the question. Had this been within a personal context it would have sounded fine, but in a job interview it sounded awful. They rephrased the question but to me it still sounded similar to the previously posed one, so I asked, 'How does this question differ from the previous one?' At that time I was tense, I needed time to think about my reply, but since I wasn't face to face with the committee of interviewers they couldn't see my expression, gestures, and body language, and couldn't quite know I was nervous, so I appeared to them as curt, and rather rude. They thought I was questioning the legitimacy of their question. And that was purely at a linguistic level. I couldn't articulate what I wanted to say; basically I couldn't reply because it wasn't my area of expertise and I needed more time to elaborate on the answer without sounding dilettantish. I came across as rude and defensive. The way I expressed my reply didn't help at all."

I'd like to clarify that Lina speaks perfect English and her difficulty in expressing herself in this particular situation within Anglo-Saxon culture relates more to the subtlety in the use of language than to the lack of appropriate words. She herself recognizes that distinction, "Even knowing that English is politer—that Americans beat around the bush a lot and that it's more elegant to use disclaimers—at that point in time I answered spontaneously, using a blunter Spanish way of saying things. So, on the phone I was perceived as an arrogant person, questioning the interviewer's query. In truth, I was really wondering why they were asking that question and how I could buy some time to answer appropriately."

Each of us sees the world through the lens of our distinctions. We then apply our opinions and emotions to the facts we observe according to the sequence I shared with you earlier, creating our own story about what really took place. As we've already seen, all the stories we make up in order to give meaning to any situation or to understand the people in our lives are created in language, which gives you tremendous power to effect change.

The Declarative Function of Language

The most creative function of language is the *declarative* one.[4] What is a declaration? It is an act of speech whereby the speaker creates a world of possibilities out of nothing. Think about the declaration of independence, American colonies declared themselves independent from Great Britain, Spain, and Portugal. This declaration doesn't describe a situation but rather creates a new

---

4. *Language and the Pursuit of Happiness*, Chalmers Brothers. New Possibilities Press, 2005.

one. Think about what happens when a judge declares two individuals "husband and wife." He's creating a legal entity between them.

The same holds true when you say yes to a job promotion; you create an employment experience inexistent until then. In turn, when you say no to the idea of opening your own company in order to continue working as an employee, you deny yourself the possibility of exploring a whole new area you're passionate about and where you could grow much more than in your routine job. Declarations create a change of context.

Valuable Declarations to Create a New Future

Typically, those who make significant changes in their lives start off with a personal declaration and a new way of seeing themselves: I'm a successful woman. I'm able to accomplish everything I set out to do. I create my own destiny. And then they use specific declarations to open, close, solve or assess opportunities. For example:

> ➢ *I don't know.* Admitting (declaring) you don't know something opens doors to learning; to acquire new distinctions which you lack and that may help you see the world from a totally different angle.
> ➢ *I forgive you.* This phrase dissolves any resentment and provides closure with the past. It's very useful to use this declaration to forgive your parents or loved ones who have contributed early on with messages that negatively impacted you, and that even today make growth difficult.
> ➢ *I'm sorry.* Declaring your responsibility regarding something that happened in the past allows you to begin a new page in that relationship.

> *Thank you.* Acknowledging others' generosity opens the possibility of accepting help and enjoyment.

> *This is not working.* This states a breakaway from the way things have been happening and leads to accepting the need to create new actions which, in turn, lead to new results.

Why Language Is the Key

Why is it so important to understand how language works in a book aimed at helping you attain your professional aspirations? Here's a list of reasons:

> Understanding that many of the reasons you claim for not achieving this or that are excuses created in language. For example, "I'm afraid of letting my bosses down" or "I'm stuck and don't know where to start" or "I don't like speaking in public" or "I'm afraid that if I grow my small business, I'll lose control."

> Understanding you have your individual communication style. We'll go further into this later on in the book. Latinos often add much more context when speaking, and we women typically use tag questions to end a statement which in fact weakens the statement and creates the perception that we're not prepared for leadership.

> Understanding that when saying (or receiving a) "no" we're not rejecting someone but simply declining a request. The request and the person are two separate stories. If you're able to make that distinction, saying no will be much easier and will help you avoid commitments you know beforehand you won't be able to fulfill.

➢ Understanding there are certain concepts (distinctions) many women didn't know about while growing up. For example, Elizabeth Nieto, Chief Diversity and Inclusion Officer at MetLife states, "Like many women, I was uncomfortable with the word ambition when I was a child. Now that I feel more comfortable stating 'I'm ambitious,' I can say I probably always was. Before I wasn't aware of it because I wasn't concerned with personal ambition rather with pleasing others, getting good grades, etc. As a grown-up I realize I no longer care about other people's expectations; I do it for myself. What's very clear to me is that I've never wanted to be number two, though in the past I found it hard to verbalize."

➢ Understanding that just as you create stories about each person you know based on what you perceive of them, the rest of the world creates a story about you. You just can't avoid it. The only thing you can control are the elements with which others will create the story. There lies the importance of your image, your communication style, your values, reputation, everything that builds your personal brand.

➢ Understanding that language has the power to create realities allows you to deconstruct a few that are no longer useful (old stories others created about you and that you believed at some point in time, like in the case of Alice) in order to make up the reality you wish for your future.

Don't you feel you've grown wings and are ready to fly?

Chapter 4

Define Your Own Journey

and Establish Your Brand

Famous Women Speak: Elena Roger

Elena Roger is the first Argentine actress to star in *Evita* on Broadway. When in 2006 she burst onto the world stage to critical acclaim for her performance as Evita Perón in the West End revival of the production, she would later go on to grab the title role in Donmar Warehouse's production of *Piaf* for which she was awarded the 2009 Laurence Olivier Award for best actress in a musical for her portrayal of Edith Piaf. Elena toured internationally with *Piaf*, and while in Buenos Aires she revived and starred in another successful musical she cocreated, *Mina . . . che cosa sei?* Throughout her career, Elena has always made sure that her next role was more challenging than the previous one. She has always looked for ways to stretch her comfort zone and to try something new. She exudes a level of confidence that is hard to miss and that has allowed her to stay true to herself despite international fame.

Q: *Looking back, can you identify some early family mandates and expectations of you that helped mold your career?*

A: Nobody told me "this is the way it has to be." My parents sent me to take dance and singing lessons because I asked them to, and my mom, seeing that I admired certain actressess, would make comments such as, "Look at her, I love how well she talks, how much she reads . . ." I think it was her way of pointing out that those were valuable things. It was an education. She never told me, "You have to read." I'm grateful because my mom never made me feel that I had to be anyone else than who I was. She never told me, "You have to get a nose job." It's funny because years later, my dad's friend told me that my dad had once confessed to him, "I'm concerned because my youngest wants to be an artist." I thought it was so sweet that he had never said that to me.

Q: *What are some of the dreams you had for yourself very early on? Have you fulfilled them all?*

A: When I realized what it felt like to work in the theater, I knew that's what I wanted to be doing all the time. I wanted to be successful in a manner that meant always having work. And I think I've fulfilled the dream of constantly doing something that is a bit more challenging than what I did before.

Q: *So what is success for you?*

A: Being happy with my life. I feel that a lot of people think they'll be happy if they have money or are famous or sign autographs, but for me it's about being happy with what you have. I feel that life is not only about professional success but also what you want of the world around you . . . how you enjoy nature, your family, your friends, your partner, if that's something that makes you happy.

Q: *Growing up in a country like Argentina where aesthetics are so important, it must have been hard to stick to your decision of not having plastic surgery. How did you manage to resist the peer pressure or even producer and agents' recommendations?*

A: It was a joke in my family to laugh at our family's defects but the joke always ended with a warning, "Don't you ever get a nose job." My nose identified me as Italian and I was proud of that heritage. I adored my grandma. But I was also a clown, so not being pretty always helped. And on the other hand, I was loved and respected by my group, I was a confident person, I always found positive things about who I was. I had big calves like my dad, and I was small-framed like my grandma. She would tell me stories about herself when she was young and point out how men liked small women. (The director who suggested that with my height I'd never land a leading role . . . well, he knows about my career trajectory.) I think women are slaves to the idea of who they are expected to be. Men have it easier. I personally need to carry light baggage so I'm faithful to who I always was. I don't wear makeup, I don't color my hair (unless I have to do it for work), I don't wear any jewelry, I just wear jeans and flats.

Q: *Well, that's exactly one of the things everyone notices about you, that despite your fame, you remain a very accessible, girl-next-door kind of woman. How do you manage to keep your head straight? Has fame changed you in ways that are not so visible to others?*

A: I had to learn how to be well known, how to deal with exhaustion, and give interviews right after a show. Sometimes, answering the same questions time and again makes your head explode. I needed to be by myself for two hours before I would speak to anyone. I had to learn to control my mood. Eventually, I understood that artists are an example for many people who read and watch these interviews. So I had to make peace with that and learn to relax. In the beginning I wasn't that great, I was very formal, I would dress up and wear makeup. But then I made the decision about the journey that I wanted to follow as a person and that's when I resolved that I would continue to be myself off the stage.

Q: *You are in a very competitive field. How has it been to work with other women and occasionally for other women? Do you have some strategies that help you get along with them?*

A: Criticizing and judging what other women do is a bad habit many people have. We forget that women have a life and you never know what circumstances made people act in a way that irritates you. I think people in general should try to be more understanding and tolerant with each other. So if someone acts poorly, instead of jumping in and creating more discord, we should ask questions and try to understand why this person acted in a certain way. It's also good to know that each one of us has an important place in this life and nobody is going to take it away from you.

Q: *Have there been times when you thought you should do X while most people thought you should do Y? What strategy did you use to stand your ground when others were not supportive of your choice?*

A: I used to ask around a lot, trying to learn from different points of view. As I get older and more secure in my career, I make most of the decisions on my own. And when I'm sure about something and someone gives me an opinion that makes me insecure, I stop them in their tracks.

How to Get Started

Let's now gather all the concepts we've been discussing and bring them into the workplace in order to focus on your intention. When we talk about verbal and nonverbal messages conveyed at work we shouldn't forget to mention your brand. I'm sure you've heard of the importance of establishing your personal brand; this concept has been around for several years now. Yet, when I present at conferences, I always notice that the majority of the participants haven't done much to enhance their own brands. For one, it's easy to become immune to the latest fad in the workplace. On the other hand, if you don't have someone to guide you on how to develop your brand, you'll have a hard time working on it at a two-hour seminar or by occasionally reading a blog.

If you're well into your career, you've probably received advice about branding at work or may have already established a well-known brand. In that case, review these suggestions and see which to apply, because if you're ready to go to the next level, you'll need to have a flawless brand first.

What Is Branding?

Branding is the word or phrase we want others to identify us with. It relates to the value you bring to the table, what makes you unique and different. For example: Maria is a fair leader, Ana is a top-notch communicator, Paula is a visionary executive. The core issue is to understand that branding has to do with the perception others have of you; a perception, as said earlier, is reality in the eye of the beholder. In other words, if your bosses perceive you've got the potential to take on a position of greater responsibility, they'll offer you that special training course that will ultimately open doors. If, on the other hand, they perceive you're not interested in growing professionally, they won't offer it to you. And maybe you *are* interested but you're not projecting the right signals; you're not clearly conveying the value you have to offer to be in your bosses' lookout. Or maybe you're not so sure about what you have to offer and what you're looking for.

Remember that in the majority of cases a person with good branding, but little talent, has more chances than someone with poor branding and much talent. And, of course, the person that's talented *and* has good branding will be better off than the rest.

Before you begin to explore your own brand, you must know that as a female (and as a minority) certain stereotypes establish a branding that precedes your decision to create your own brand. For instance, before Maria is known as a fair leader she's perceived as a Hispanic woman, and people may assume she's passionate, has a high degree of empathy, prioritizes her personal life over her job, etc. These are all assumptions (or stories people tell themselves about Maria) that may or may not be true in Maria's particular case, but that she'll nevertheless have to overcome when building her own leadership brand. Above all, Maria wants to be known as a fair leader.

The first step to explore is what phrase (and reality) you want to be appreciated for, and if it doesn't match the perception others have of you right now, you have two options: 1) you either adjust your behavior, physical appearance or relationships (I'll provide details later on); or 2) you adjust your brand.

What Aspects Must You Consider in Your Branding?

Think of your favorite clothing brand. Surely you're familiar with their logo, colors, and slogan. You also know the style of clothing that brand offers very well. Let's say it's classic, innovative, high-quality, and projects the image of a successful female professional. Imagine if your favorite brand unexpectedly decided to change its look to focus on the teen market. Not only do its designs change, its quality declines. Would you continue buying that brand? Probably not. So you see, there are many elements that make you buy and trust a brand. The same goes for your personal brand.

♥ ♥ ♥ ♥ ♥

How Do You Define Your Brand?

Before defining your brand you must explore the image you currently project. Then decide whether it serves your interests or if you'd rather project something different in the future. You can start the process by exploring the following steps:

- Make a list of adjectives you believe define you. For example, hardworking, diligent, innovative, organized, etc.
- Ask your trusted acquaintances and colleagues to mention a few adjectives they believe define you. (In my experience, it's best to ask them to send their answers via email instead of telling you in person. This option allows people to tell you things they probably wouldn't say in person.)
- Compare both lists. Do they match?
- If not, you must assess the reason. Are you far removed from reality? Are you not objective enough about your weaknesses or, on the contrary, are you too critical of yourself? Does the person who's evaluating you only know you in a specific environment which limits his/her opinion to that small aspect of your life? Are you able to adjust some part of your behavior to change what others perceive about you? Oftentimes, we'd like to be what we aren't, and try to change to adapt to what we wish to emulate, only to distance ourselves further from our authentic self. Remember, a perceived lack of authenticity is not appreciated. If this is the case, you're better off adjusting your expectations in terms of what you want your brand to be.
- For example, Gladys has the ideal voice, style, and repertoire to be an opera singer. But she wants to be the new Shakira. When she received feedback from her advisory team they told her she was "the next Maria Callas." A letdown for Gladys because she would've liked to be told she'd be the next Shakira. Given her talent and profile, the chances of changing others' perception of her are limited. She'd be better off aligning her expectations to a

brand that naturally relates to her talent and to what others see as well.

Remember, it will be hard to force your branding when it doesn't naturally align with your personality, values, talent or expertise.

♠   ♠   ♠   ♠   ♠

Use this sheet below to list the adjectives and phrases you believe identify you. In the second column add feedback from friends and colleagues.

What I think	What others think	✓ Agreement

Once you've decided on the branding you want to be known for, make sure all the elements that make up your image are consistent with your brand.

When I launched my career as a writer and speaker, I went through a similar exercise illustrated above. I hired a professional photographer who took five hundred photos of me. I picked only ten and sent them to a group of colleagues I trust blindly (my "board of advisors") to help me choose the one for my brand image. They answered candidly: *This looks too childish*; *This one is too naïve*; *In this one you look too sexy*; *This one projects openness, an interest in listening to what others have to say, i.e., you look like someone I could relate to and tell my problems*. Evidently, that last picture ended up on my website, business cards, stationery letterhead, etc. A designer worked on the colors that best represented my energy and purpose. And after several sessions with this group of professionals I found the adjectives that represent me: dynamic, open, honest, a good communicator, and an excellent networker.

Feedback

The problem is that sometimes you inadvertently send conflicting messages. You want to be like Shakira yet you record operas. You want to be a manager but when offered the chance to lead other employees you reject it. You're struggling to get that big contract from a multinational company but fail to comply with delivery dates for a smaller project they entrusted you with and lose credibility. That's why it's so important to listen to feedback from your colleagues, bosses, and acquaintances. For Janet Wigfield, Executive Vice President and Conference and Events Director at Working Mother Media, getting honest feedback from people she works with about her performance has been critical for her career development: "That feedback is sometimes formal or through how an event went. On a couple of occasions I worked with executive coaches to help me take a better look at what I want."

The difficulty for many women (and men) of Hispanic descent is that they find it hard to listen to feedback. They take it so much to heart that listening to negative feedback makes them feel they're being rejected. Their need to be liked by others interferes with their ability to listen to what others think to such an extent, they often prefer not to ask and simply bury their heads in the sand.

Another kind of behavior I've observed among certain ethnic/cultural groups when receiving feedback, is that they often act defensively and seize the moment to give their own opinion about what the other person should change about themselves. I've experienced this myself and I can assure you there's no better way to deter me from offering someone feedback than that.

However, it's important to make a clear distinction here: when you react defensively and someone tells you "don't take it personally," they're not saying your feelings aren't legitimate. They're really telling you to take some distance from the situation in order not to feel so affected and be able to recognize that the feedback given (or the way you were treated) wasn't against you at all. I recently had a lengthy discussion with my friend David García, director and trainer at Dynamic Fitness gym. He complained about his clients' constant whining when they come to the gym (I don't feel like being here, I don't feel like training, etc.) and about how they don't pay attention to his instructions. For David, who wanted his clients to get their money's worth, hearing this feedback put him in a bad mood. I (and others before me) told him to not take it personally. It's like the dentist's office, everybody hates going to the dentist, but it's nothing against the poor dentist. The same here. People find it hard to make the effort to train, they don't like to have to go through muscle pain, the sweating, etc. It's really nothing against David.

After thirty minutes in this heated discussion I realized that when I had told David to not take things personally, he understood that I was telling him he had no reason to let people's attitudes upset him. To clear up the misunderstanding I said, "David, you're absolutely right in feeling upset about people's bad vibes, for being disrespectful of your time when they don't sign up for their spinning class ahead of time, or when they don't follow your instructions. But I suggest you focus on the priority of running a profitable business, and instead of being stuck on who's right and who's wrong, or let comments faze you, focus on your goals." The atmosphere immediately changed between us. David felt heard and validated and I understood these words had a totally different meaning for him than for me. That's why it's so important we all recognize these small distinctions that can really make a huge difference in various aspects of our careers and personal lives.

I learned a long time ago that the only way to grow is by putting the ego aside.

The great Mexican writer Elena Poniatowska told me, "I never had an ego. I have no problem cutting out what doesn't work in my books. I don't defend my writings." Think of how strong these words are for a writer and you'll see that surely part of the reason for her great success is not having an excessive attachment to what she produces. She's disconnected her identity from her work to such a degree that when an editor suggests cutting out ten pages she can do so humbly while remaining focused on her final goal of publishing the best book possible. That is to say, she clearly understands that words must be used (or removed) to her own benefit.

While we're on the subject of words, what we do with them and what results we obtain with their usage, may differ from one person to the next. For instance another writer who is told, "you must delete one hundred pages because the book is too long," might think, *oh, that means I'm a poor writer* and may get depressed. And yet another might react by saying: "Hey, who do you think you are telling me how I must write my book? You're telling *me*? You're the one who keeps sending me mile-long emails every time you need to ask me something." Now I ask you: What sorts of results do you think these last two writers get?" They're likely to be very different than those achieved by Elena Poniatowska.

Consider the fact that you're not just your ego. For example, I won't fall apart as a person just because someone tells me I have to speak slower when I present or must wear this or that outfit to lecture in front of corporate executives. On the contrary, I believe, like Janet Wigfield, that the reasons I grew so much in my profession had to do with always seeking others' feedback, being open, and admitting I don't know it all.

The "Attraction" Factor

Some studies[1] show that attractive people earn 10% more and have greater opportunities. The fact that they're attractive subconsciously communicates to others that they're good and productive at what they do. But don't be afraid, being attractive doesn't mean that if you're not lucky enough to be naturally stunning, six feet tall, and wear a size one, you're in trouble. Any of us can become attractive, but first we must think about the attitude we project. For example, self-confidence is a very attractive quality. As is generosity, joy, optimism, and other virtues that brighten your life and the lives of those who get to know you. A good attitude coupled with looks, spotless manners, a reputation that precedes you, and a good communication style may turn you into the most attractive woman on earth.

Three Aspects That Make Up Your Brand

To make it easy for you to examine your present image and get to know yourself better, we'll explore a brand's three main aspects:

1. "Beauty and the Labor Market," Dr. Daniel Hamermesh and Jeff E. Biddle. *The American Economic Review*, 1994.

> Physical appearance and collateral materials
> Behavior, attitude, and values
> Personal relationships

Physical Appearance and Collateral Materials

This aspect includes both your physical appearance as well as all the materials you use to identify yourself or promote your activities. Some examples:

> Clothing and accessories
> Makeup
> Perfume and scents
> Personal grooming, hairstyle, and nails
> Business cards and stationery
> Brochures
> Website/ social networks

Behavior, Attitude, and Values

This aspect includes nonverbal communication, your values, personality traits, and how you interact with others. Some examples:

> How you walk
> Your communication style
> Your voice: tone, volume
> Your eating manners, how you hold a pen, say please, and thank you
> Conversation topics
> If you work well as part of a team or if you'd rather work alone
> If you're generous or selfish
> If you keep your word or are unreliable

> ➢ If you treat your subordinates well
> ➢ If you are humble or arrogant
> ➢ If you are punctual
> ➢ Your creativity level

Personal Relationships

Your reputation is impacted, either positively or negatively, by the people you surround yourself with. If you're around well-respected and highly competent people, they'll surely have a positive impact on your image. If, on the other hand, you surround yourself with people known to be unreliable, the outcome will be negative. Some examples:

> ➢ Who your friends are
> ➢ Who is listed in your professional network
> ➢ Who you relate to in the workplace
> ➢ Who you attract
> ➢ Who you refer to in public

THE VOICE OF EXPERIENCE

"Surround yourself with queens and ask them as many questions as possible. Observe who is doing the right thing and follow along that path. Ultimately, kings and queens like to talk to other kings and queens."
—Pamela Ravare-Jones, Director of Operations at ALPFA, the Association of Hispanic Professionals in Accounting and Finance

----

What Comes Next?

This is the time to grab a pencil and paper or sit down in front of your computer and harness your thoughts on branding. Start by reviewing and examining each item on the list. The idea is to score each item on a scale from 1 to 5 (1 being the lowest) to get an x-ray of your current brand and focus on your weakest points. This will also help you find specific coaches to continue with your development. (I'll be discussing what an advisory board is and how to create one later on.)

Once you've completed the exercise further below, I suggest you send a fresh copy of this same form via email to a select group of friends and colleagues to get feedback, just as you did before to find out about what adjectives best represent who you are. Get ready to listen to some things you might not want to hear, or to discover some differences between your self-perception and the perception others have of you. These might be good areas for improvement. If you're open to constructive criticism, you'll substantially reduce the time it'll take you to make those changes and you'll achieve your goals faster. For example, if your intention is to improve your brand to project an image of a professional woman ready to lead the marketing department, you must listen to the comments your colleagues send you as if they were gifts that'll help you materialize your intention in less time. Therefore, be sure your criticism filters don't end up creating unproductive stories. And whenever necessary, tone down your inner voice if you notice it's getting out of hand.

♥　♥　♥　♥　♥

Note for Requesting Feedback

When sending the feedback request sheet to your trusted friends and colleagues, include a brief explanatory note along these lines:

Hi,

I'm working on my brand and would like to ask your opinion on some aspects that may have an impact on my career development. I would greatly appreciate if you would take a few minutes to score on a scale from 1 to 5 (1 being the lowest) the list of items attached. I'd also appreciate your comments on how you think I may improve those items where the score is 3 or less. For example, if you assign a "2" on the clothing and accessories item, you might add something like, "try dressing less casual" or any other helpful comment.

Thanks in advance!

♠   ♠   ♠   ♠   ♠

Circle the score for each item on the list below, 1 being the lowest score.

Clothing and accessories	1	2	3	4	5
Makeup	1	2	3	4	5
Perfume and scents	1	2	3	4	5
Personal grooming, hairstyle, and nails	1	2	3	4	5
Business cards and stationery	1	2	3	4	5
Brochures	1	2	3	4	5
Website/social networks	1	2	3	4	5
Way of walking	1	2	3	4	5
Communication style	1	2	3	4	5
Voice: Tone/volume/pitch	1	2	3	4	5
Table manners	1	2	3	4	5
Manners in general	1	2	3	4	5
Conversation topics	1	2	3	4	5
Teamwork	1	2	3	4	5
Generosity	1	2	3	4	5
Reliability	1	2	3	4	5
Treating subordinates	1	2	3	4	5
Humbleness	1	2	3	4	5
Being on time	1	2	3	4	5

Commitment to work	1	2	3	4	5
Dedication	1	2	3	4	5
My friends	1	2	3	4	5
My contacts	1	2	3	4	5
People I attract	1	2	3	4	5

How to Effect Change

Once you receive the feedback, put together all the answers and observe the areas where there's agreement between your friends and colleagues. For instance, if several of them believe there's room to improve on your communication style, take note of it and explore it further. In other words, ask them for specific descriptions about the way you speak that will enable you to understand what you should work on. Have a telephone or face-to-face conversation with them and find out whether they have any specific recommendations for you to work on or if they're familiar with a coach or expert who can help you make the necessary adjustments.

You should also take into account those areas where you scored 4 or 5 and make sure you benefit from them. For example, if everyone thinks you have an excellent group of friends and contacts, then continue expanding your circle.

Lastly, if only one person assigns a low score to one of the items and the rest are all high scores, it could be that person hasn't had the chance to see you under those circumstances or has shared a particular experience with you. For example, if someone assigns a 1 for "general manners" and you've scored 4 or 5 with the rest, that person may recall a team meeting where you interrupted their presentation in front of their supervisor. If you know the reason for discrepancy on a specific score, tap into it, and remind yourself not to neglect those details. If you're unaware of the reason, ask that person directly.

How to Talk about Yourself

When you meet someone for the first time it's critical to have a clear picture of your brand. How do you introduce yourself? What details do you choose to share? It's not the same if I say, "hello, I'm Mariela Dabbah, author, speaker, and consultant on issues that help Latinos be successful through education, professional development, and empowerment," versus "hello, I'm Mariela Dabbah, I live in Westchester, New York." I could also take that moment to connect further with them by saying, "hello, I'm Mariela Dabbah, writer and speaker. I'd like to ask you a few questions for the book I'm working on." And although my introduction (and yours) varies according to the situation at hand and one's career stage, I deliberately decide what to say in which context rather than letting the context surprise me leaving me speechless. The work you've done so far in defining your brand based on your aspirations will help you find those words.

In addition to introductory phrases, I'd like you to consider how you talk about yourself, what you say during your conversations with people you've just met, and with colleagues you interact with daily. As we've been discussing, human relationships are built on communication. Through language you let others know what your goals are and by using the right language you can align your words to your actions to ultimately attain your goals. What you say about yourself has a direct impact on how others react to you, and whether they'll help you achieve your goals. As you build your brand it's critical to self-assess your use of this delicate tool to foster and keep those relationships. It's also important to acknowledge that as you're promoted to positions demanding greater responsibility, you'll have to adjust your communication style and what you say about yourself.

Minding language is critical for everyone, but women must pay special attention not to pick up bad habits that are detrimental when attempting to achieve our goals. I'll be talking about this in further detail in my next chapter on communication. Here's a preview of some important points to consider when speaking about yourself:

> Limit the amount of personal information you share with your colleagues
> Limit the amount of context you offer in your conversations
> Find the most direct way to say what you want to say—without being aggressive
> Tone down your emotions
> Learn how to speak about your personal achievements and the team you lead
> Ask for what you want and support your request with objective and relevant data

Now that you have all this valuable feedback available to work on your brand, ideally you should find mentors to help you in specific areas (in later chapters I'll discuss how valuable mentors are for your growth). After you've spent quality time making all the necessary adjustments, send the form back to your group of friends to see how their perception about you has changed. What's most important, however, is for you yourself to observe how much better your brand relates to what you envision for your future.

Remember that once your brand is well defined you should tap into it to achieve greater visibility. Go ahead and dare to express your goals, points of view, opinions, and achievements with greater clarity whenever you get the chance. Don't keep quiet and wait for someone to appreciate your hard work or the legitimacy of your ideas. We'll talk more in depth about this further on in the book.

Arturo Poiré's Corner

✦

"You've got to be careful not to go from a meek, submissive, undemanding-type style to an aggressive one with unrealistic demands. Once, a CFO of a large corporation remarked on the radical change she had observed in Rosalind, an employee for whom she had high regard. Rosalind had always been well respected on her team, but she was also very passive in terms of her career. During her midyear performance review the CFO suggested several possible roads. Rosalind suddenly realized there was a position she had always aspired to: she wanted to be the company's treasurer. Shortly after, she requested another meeting with the CFO where she pressured her for that position using arguments like, 'I should've been in that position years ago.' The CFO, who had considered Rosalind as a possible candidate for that position, began to hesitate about her skills and maturity. She discovered someone who was incapable of controlling her emotions, because the reality was the position wasn't open years back; some organizational adjustments had to be made before Rosalind could be considered for that post. You must be careful not to go from being a meek person to a super ambitious one. If it suddenly dawns on you that there's something you want, you can't just go full speed trying to recoup lost time. You must carefully plan how to get there, and maybe hire a coach to help you out. There are ways to shorten the time frame."

Chapter 5

Decide and Plan Your Future

Famous Women Speak: María Elena Salinas

As coanchor of "Noticiero Univision" since 1987, she's one the most recognized and influential female journalists in Spanish-language media. She's interviewed some of the world's most powerful people, including Presidents Barack Obama, Bill Clinton and Jimmy Carter, and has received numerous awards including an Emmy in 1999. Born in California to Mexican parents, María Elena started her career in journalism in 1981 as a reporter for KMEX-34 in Los Angeles. By covering stories that resonated well with the Hispanic community, she quickly gained the public's trust and a seat at the leading news program for U.S. Latinos. She's one of the hardest working people I know in this medium and is always ready to lend a hand to those who come behind her.

Q: *What does success mean to you? How do you define it?*

A: Success is very relative. Some believe it means to achieve an important position, earn a lot of money or to be famous. Yet I believe that success is attained when we each get to fulfill our own goals, no matter how big or small they may be.

Q: *As a Latina in a male-dominated world, what have been some of the strategies you've used to assure you're heard?*

A: First of all, I've worked twice as much as men. Though we'd like to believe that male chauvinism is something of the past, unfortunately women still have to work twice as much as men to earn half the recognition for their work. But it's important to do it wholeheartedly. Luckily, I'm not afraid of work; it doesn't bother me in the least to have to work harder to show I can do what a man does. And as I like to say, better still because we get to wear high heels. It's also essential to establish good communication with your colleagues and bosses. It's important to ask when there's something you want, offer your help, and complain diplomatically when something is not right.

Q: *One of the great challenges for women is learning how to negotiate what they truly deserve. How much do you participate in negotiations done on your behalf? Do you find you've benefited as a woman in delegating that role to a man?*

A: I work at a place that has been a matriarchy for years. All bosses were female. From the very beginning it was established that my male counterpart, Jorge Ramos, and myself would be treated equally, and that we would share responsibilities in the news department. Some of those responsibilities are ensured by contract. My legal representatives for contract negotiations are, by chance, men. Yet a woman could have very well been in charge of those negotiations.

Q: *Do you believe your industry has different requirements and expectation levels for women in comparison to men?*

A: In my industry I believe they are equal. As journalists, we all have to be equally prepared to cover any news story and be available when we're called for special coverage or to travel somewhere. It is harder for women, especially when we're mothers, and it's even more complicated when you're a single mother like me. But a good way of proving we're equal is searching for solutions when things get complicated at home. There was a time when it was believed that only men could cover a war, for example, but things have changed. Women can also do it, and, at times, with greater sensitivity.

Q: *What advice can you offer ambitious Latinas?*

A: I've always believed that the worst obstacle to self-improvement is that which we have in our minds. Insecurity, shyness, and holding a grudge are our worst enemies. So we must first believe in ourselves and in our ability to do anything we set out to do. We must also be careful not to complain too much when things don't work out the way we want them to because that's exactly what men expect from us. The best way to excel is through our work, not by complaining. Fortunately, this is a generation where women have shown they can do and be anything they want: reaching for the presidency, the Supreme Court, running large corporations, traveling into space, and at the same time being in charge of our home, being mothers, and wives.

Q: *On a scale from 1 to 5 (1 being the lowest) do you consider yourself:*

a. Risk taker: 5
b. Competitive: 4
c. Ambitious: 3

A: For me it's important to do things well, but I'm not competing with anybody on a personal level. My company is competitive and our program competes with other networks' programs, but I personally am not competitive. My only ambition is not to be a conformist and not to allow myself to be mediocre. One thing is for sure, I would like to be the best mother in the world!

Putting into practice the process you started a few chapters back could take a few months. It's not easy to become aware of messages and beliefs deeply rooted in your mind from very early on that seem normal to you. So much so, you may not realize that the aversion you have to communicate your achievements may be related to old beliefs such as "girls cannot stand out more than boys" or "girls must be seen but not heard" or to your religion's vow of humility. Be patient with yourself.

The first step is acknowledging how far you've come. Once you assess your assumptions from the past and recognize them as a result of some early event which you chose to view in a certain way (consciously or unconsciously) the rest becomes second nature. As a result, such assumptions will no longer be so transparent and you'll be able to declare a new reality which in turn will help you achieve new results. What do I mean by transparent? Think of how many times you drive to work without even realizing what road you take. Or when you get on a bike and ride alongside a friend chatting away without having to think about how to pedal. Or the breath you take in and later exhale? If you were aware, you wouldn't be doing anything but breathing! Activities such as driving, riding a bike or breathing have become transparent to you. You do them automatically. That's why you're often unaware of the amount of functions your body and brain are actually performing. The same holds true with the use of language. Since you can't break away from it, your thoughts use it all the time. You forget that your actions are based on what you think of yourself, and that a good part of those beliefs were shaped early on in your life. To move to a higher plain it's critical for those beliefs to become visible. That is, they must shift from the state of transparency they dwell in now.

One of those unquestioned beliefs—so deeply rooted you aren't even sure of its origin—is the avoidance of long-term planning.

The Latino culture tends to be what researchers call a *polychronic* culture, i.e., seeing the world holistically and considering time as a continuum. In contrast, the Anglo-Saxon culture is *monochronic* and sees time as sequential and compartmentalized.[1] The polychron is often late due to the manner in which they see time. Exact times are not really meaningful. The monochron, who is kept waiting for the polychron, cannot fathom such tardiness. While the polychron was tidying up her home just before leaving for the appointment, the monochron was already at the appointed place five minutes early and staring at the clock. In the U.S. many have experienced this clash of worldviews. If you don't appreciate the different concepts of time between Latinos and non-Latinos, you'll be dragging this problem around for years.

Along the same lines, the lack of long-term planning may be related to the high degree of uncertainty pervasive in the region you come from. When you've gone through enough coups, government expropriations of private property, corruption, guerilla warfare, rampant inflation, currency devaluation, and many of the other difficulties Latin America has undergone, you get used to living short-term and not planning more than a few months ahead. But if you live in the U.S. or any other developed country, you must recognize that lack of planning will affect your career growth possibilities. Therefore, you must acquire the necessary tools so that you will feel comfortable planning.

Lastly, think about the ubiquitous Latin American expression *Si Dios quiere* or "God willing." For the majority of us, including this phrase in any future plan which, unconsciously, poses the notion that what happens is not in our hands, comes out spontaneously. For example: *See you tomorrow, God willing* or *God willing,*

1. *The Dance of Life: The Other Dimension of Time*, E.T. Hall. Anchor Press/Doubleday, 1983.

we'll be launching this new project in the upcoming month. And though it's sensible to consider contingencies, we might be overly emphasizing our lack of personal control over things. Be aware of how you use this expression so it's no longer transparent and you're able to observe its impact on your planning skills.

♥   ♥   ♥   ♥   ♥

Remember Your Advantage

There's also a highly positive side to the circumstances you were brought up in a Latino household. As Arturo Poiré and I mentioned in our book *The Latino Advantage in the Workplace* (Sourcebooks, 2007), Latinos are known for their adaptability and creative problem-solving skills. But the fact that you're able to adjust to any sudden change and find a solution, while others tend to make a mountain out of a molehill, is transparent to you. During a financial crisis, you're probably the person who comes up with the best ideas on how to save money, lower costs, and increase production with less investment. It's also possible that you may view these traits, which are second nature to you, as nothing special. The truth is they are your advantage as a Latina (and, most likely, as a person raised in any developing country). So, it's critical to make these traits visible to yourself and others in order to leverage them to your benefit.

♠   ♠   ♠   ♠   ♠

How to Get Started

Now it's time to gather the material on aspirations you've been exploring throughout these pages and project them into the future. Bring forth that image, that dream of who you want to be in the future, the dream you arrived at after doing your visualization exercises. It's important to write that goal on a calendar. How many years from now do you want to be that woman? To make it clear, I'll use an example.

Mercedes Sánchez is the founder of the beauty and fashion blog, Bechicmag.com. She started her digital magazine in 2006 and managed it simultaneously while working for Adolfo Carrión, the Bronx Borough President. A few years back, due to staff cuts she lost her job. So Mercedes turned her focus to her blog. She decided that her dream was to make a living from this project. But in order to do so she needed to look for sponsors to grow her business. Her goal was to achieve her dream in two years' time. If we were in Mercedes' shoes, the idea now would be to start from that desired date (two years) and work backwards. First, by creating milestones she must achieve in the months to come and second, by defining specific actions to accomplish those established milestones.

Goal Planning Sheets

Below are a few tables to help you write down your aspirations so that you can commit yourself to meeting them.

The Goal

Clearly define your goals, the intended timeframe to meet them, and the measuring method you'll be using to confirm completion. For instance, Mercedes' goal is to earn $60,000 a year from her online magazine.

Goal	I intend to meet it by	How I'll measure success

Factors That Will Influence Goal Completion

Identify the factors that will directly contribute to meeting your goal. For example, Mercedes will need a visible brand, good online traffic, and several media partnerships to disseminate her platform, and therefore attract interested sponsors. How she'll measure each factor will vary. For instance, she'd like fifty thousand single monthly visits to her blog to attract the attention of companies interested in her market segment.

Factors impacting on goal	How I'll measure success	I intend to meet my goal by

Actions I Must Implement to Fulfill Factors Leading to Goal Achievement

Here's where you explain what actions you must carry out in order to meet each of the factors listed above. I suggest using a similar sheet for each factor. For instance, Mercedes could decide that in order to reach fifty thousand single monthly visits, the first step would be to partner with several media platforms relevant to her readership. She'll therefore list each platform and include the date by which she'd like to establish partnerships. She must obviously consider imponderables. Maybe not all the companies she's interested in will want to partner with Bechicmag.com. She must therefore include additional options to resort to in case of unfavorable responses from her favorite media choices.

Actions required to meet goal	Resources I have for action	Resources needed for action	How I'll measure success	I intend to meet my goal by

This is a simple method to help you start planning your career goals. Once you start using it, you'll probably notice there are many intermediate levels I haven't referred to. For example, how will Mercedes manage to partner with leading media if she doesn't know key people? She'll have to add the step "Become a member of media associations in order to attend conferences where I can meet those required contacts" to her goal calendar. You'll need to repeat this exercise with each new element of your plan. What's most interesting about this calendar is that when you start putting things in writing and assign them dates, you send a message to your brain and environment (through words used and actions taken) so that everything aligns to your advantage. This method also helps you determine parameters you yourself set to measure your success, while enabling you to see what areas need input from others.

> ### YOUR VOICE THROUGH SOCIAL NETWORKS
>
> "Despite my initial plan of becoming an editor and working in my native tongue [Spanish], throughout my career I had to adapt and take leaps when opportunities opened up for me. Most of the time opportunities were even better than the goals I had set!"
>
> —*Miriam Fabiancic, former Editor in Chief of Mosaico Book Club, via Facebook*

If you've never formally planned your goals, you may have to sit with a coach to help you do it. Keep your mind open to suggestions as to courses or certifications required, lateral movements to acquire expertise in certain areas, memberships to associations, and any other suggestions your coach makes. Mariel Fiori, director of *La Voz* magazine, earned two separate degrees in journalism and translation in Argentina and recently finished an MBA program at New York University. "There came a time where I wanted to learn about the organizational part of journalism. I had been practicing it and learning on the go, but having structured training at a prestigious university provided me with good accreditation and credibility," says Fiori. The idea is that once you've set your long-term goal you should be able to identify the steps that lead toward it. You may not have estimated, for example, that an MBA is required to reach that managerial position you seek.

THE VOICE OF EXPERIENCE

"When I was majoring in finance, it was very upsetting to realize that I didn't like it as much as I thought I would. This was after my first official finance internship. I wanted to think out of the box, be more cutting edge, and exercise my charisma and people skills in business . . . be a marketing expert! But I was already tied (or so I thought) to a specialty I didn't really like. Now ten or fifteen years later I realize that a blend of analytical and financial skills, combined with creativity, was an excellent tool for success! So if your field is not analytical, I recommend taking some time out to sharpen your financial skills. They'll make you more powerful at decision-making, proposal-writing, and negotiating."

—*Liliana Gil, cofounder and managing partner at XL Alliance LLC*

For many women, the required steps they must take toward meeting their goals implies acquiring hard skills, i.e., quantitative skills such as financial analysis, statistics, and operations, among others. As you're projecting your future, it's a good idea to seek advice from individuals who know your trajectory, skills, interests, and training, and who, in turn, also know your industry.

Arturo Poiré's Corner
✦

"Goals can change throughout life. The good thing about having a clear long-term goal is that it can act as a guide for the actions you must take to meet it. I always recommend to the professional people I advise to identify someone who is in the position they'd like to hold. Once they've identified that person they should take a look at what makes them successful. It's important to see who's in their network, who has helped them, what kind of education and experiences they had, etc. I also suggest that they study those people's behavior, how they communicate ideas or how they perform at meetings. It's a methodical way of considering what actions to take and how you can create shortcuts to reach your destination faster. A good coach can really be helpful in doing so. What's important is knowing how long it will take to refocus on what you want to achieve, and then be realistic in terms of time and efforts needed to meet your goal. Typically, people want to get someplace or to a position *right this minute* and they're still not ready for it."

PART TWO

Tools to Grow
Your Career

Chapter 6

How to Modulate the Volume

of Your Passion

Famous Women Speak: Remedios Díaz Oliver

Remedios Díaz Oliver is one of the most powerful and admired women in the business world. Her company, All American Containers, Inc., has offices in numerous countries (Panama, Trinidad, Dominican Republic, England, and Australia, among others), and supplies containers to companies such as Coca Cola, Pepsi, Shering, and McCormick. Yet this well-known and award-winning businesswoman started out way down the ladder when she arrived in the U.S. in 1961 as a Cuban exile. Like so many, she thought she'd stay a month or two but wound up making the U.S. her new home.

Q: *How did you get involved in the male-dominated industry of manufacturing containers, plastic, glass, and metal lids?*

A: I didn't choose a male industry. When I arrived from Cuba I was young and inexperienced but I had been trained by my family who was in-volved in the education business. My parents—Spaniards—wanted me to learn a few languages. I also had tutors at home who taught me several subjects. I studied at the Havana Business Academy and Havana Business University. In addition, I took different import/export courses in Miami. I applied for a job and was offered three on the same day. But the most convenient one (since we only had one car) was a small company dedicated to the container business called Emmer Glass. When I started working I earned $55 a week for five and a half days' work. I started out as accounting assistant, and in a year's time I became vice president of the company and began the international division. I then became president and increased sales by 400% for operations conducted in Central America, South America, and the Caribbean. When the company was sold I started my own business selling glass and plastic containers for several industries: pharmaceutical, cosmetic, food, juice, and refreshments. I also sold metal (tin) containers for paint and chemical industries.

Q: *These days there are plenty of women working in male-dominated industries, but when you started out you were one of a few. How did you earn the respect of your employees, colleagues, and clients?*

A: It wasn't easy but I earned it. I used to provide additional services to clients, I'd help them with labeling; many times I translated things for them, etc. That is, I'd go the extra mile. I was the first woman in this business. At the beginning, the hardest work was in the U.S., and not in Latin America where I was always welcomed with a show of friendship, fondness, and politeness. Locally, large buyers didn't go for a young Hispanic girl. Through hard work and specializing in packaging techniques, etc., I was able to show that I was a woman who knew what I was doing and that in spite of my young age I had a sound educational background.

Q: *Throughout your career you've served on the boards of directors for several nonprofit organizations, something not enough Hispanic men and women do. Has this positively impacted your business?*

A: My work on boards of directors enabled me to expand my network.

Although it didn't help me sell more, I learned how large businesses operated. It allowed me to understand how to hire personnel, about long-range business planning, etc. That experience was very valuable. I was able to learn from and share with great businessmen and women: the Presidents/CEOs of American Airlines and Whirlpool, the Executive Vice President of Ford Motor Company, and former Vice President Dick Cheney, was on the Board of U.S. West. On Avon's Board of Directors I worked intensely with the smartest women in the cosmetic industry. I had the chance to learn about economics, funding, etc.; they were all learning experiences that proved to be very useful through the years.

Q: *Several of your family members work at All American Containers, Inc. What's the recipe for getting along well?*

A: I must say our family relations are excellent. My daughter Rosie and my granddaughter Jackie work in the sales department. My son Fausto works at creating new business opportunities and new branches. He also manages operations in California and the Midwest. My husband Fausto and I manage Miami, Tampa, Puerto Rico, and Atlanta, although we also help out in other areas. We keep a loving and respectful business relationship and try to work together for the furtherance of our operation. Each one tries to focus on an area so that we don't step on each other's toes. Our employees are part of our family and we involve them in profit-sharing plans.

One day, upon the conclusion of a workshop on how to obtain greater visibility in the workplace, a woman named Maryelena approached me and said, "I read your book *The Latino Advantage in the Workplace*, and you say that we Latinas aren't confrontational, yet I find it's the complete opposite in my case. I'm very blunt; I say what I think, and if somebody doesn't like it, that's their problem. I wouldn't dream of changing; that's the way I am. I wanted to know your thoughts about this because my boss believes I'm too aggressive and I wouldn't want this to interfere with my growth opportunities."

Maryelena is not alone. I've heard similar remarks at practically all the workshops I conduct. And I'll tell you what I tell them: The secret is not to stop being who you are but to find the point where you're most effective. If being blunt and passionate gets in the way of others listening to you, maybe you should find a way of saying what you want to say differently. It's not about silencing your viewpoint, but modulating the tool you're using to deliver that message.

Chances are you'll have to adjust your self-assessment ability so you can identify the most productive level of passion required for each occasion. In other words, be the leader of your passion instead of allowing it to lead you along paths you'll find hard to retrace.

The Art of Volume Control

I call it *art* because it's obviously not a science and you're the only one who can handle the subtleties inherent to your emotions. You're the one who knows your work environment, industry, work team, and the peculiarities of your bosses and colleagues the best. You're also familiar with how structured or flexible you can be using different communication styles with your colleagues. And like an artist you must first take your brush, choose the palette and its color intensity, the lights and shadows, and other details, to attain the work of art you desire.

Let's go back to Maryelena for a moment. She's convinced that she has the right to express herself as she pleases. She's certain that she's right and, therefore, her manager is wrong in thinking she's too confrontational. As long as she's steadfast in "being right," without prioritizing obtaining good results, it'll be difficult to move past the situation blocking her. Yet, if she could set aside her ego and focus on a new goal, i.e., achieving positive results, she'll then be able to easily adjust her communication style. In this case it would mean toning down her intensity (volume or behavior) to "sound" more rational to her boss which, in turn, will probably result in his being more receptive to her viewpoint.

THE VOICE OF EXPERIENCE

"I feel passion is a very important ingredient to add to what we do but sometimes people misinterpret it and say, 'You shouldn't be so passionate or emotional.' During one of my first presentations at Viacom, one of my bosses interrupted me and said, 'Can I ask you something? Did you drink three cups of coffee today?' I didn't feel it was a positive remark and I thought, I'd better lower the intensity a bit. There've been times when people told me, 'You're too passionate' or 'You're becoming hysterical.' Eventually, when I was being prepared for a general management position at a Spanish-language television station I was assisted by a leadership coach who showed me what my communication style was like. In order to be an effective leader, I had to adapt my style to the audience. She showed me how those same traits which made me a leader could also work against me. For example, I have a hierarchical mindset and understand how to work with my bosses. I don't need to be encouraged all the time to become motivated, but many people do, and as a manager I had to learn how to pat people on the back. If I hadn't had that coach, I wouldn't have realized these things."

—*Lucía Ballas-Traynor, cofounder of MamasLatinas.com*

I'd like to be very clear and even repetitive. I'm not suggesting abandoning the passion you bring to what you do. It's an extremely valuable trait and also reveals to others the topics you're interested in. But if you cry wolf too often, nobody will pay attention anymore. What I'm suggesting is monitoring the intensity level with which you communicate your opinions by making small adjustments to your delivery according to your audience. For instance, if you're in a meeting with a group of Latino employees, chances are the majority will express themselves within your same parameters and most will think you're not making irrational remarks. On the other hand, if you articulate those same remarks at a meeting with several non-Latino executives, they may wonder if you're coolheaded enough for the kind of critical decision-making required for the position you're being considered for. So you see, it's a question of perception and we always perceive with the unique filters of our own experience, biases, cultural backgrounds, and emotions. It doesn't really matter if your intention was not to appear irrational, unstable or rash. It only matters if the audience perceived you that way, ultimately drawing conclusions that may prove detrimental to you. It's inevitable, each audience creates their own stories about you according to their own filters.

This is not to say you should stop expressing your opinions or that you should set aside your ways. What it means it that you should control your tone in professional settings and especially outside of your community. This will facilitate creating a story that's beneficial to your goals. I know these subtleties aren't easy to implement, and you may need the help of a professional coach, as in the case of Lucía and many other women I know. Once someone directs your antennas toward these distinctions it's much easier to incorporate them naturally.

Another alternative some people find useful is taking drama lessons to specifically learn how to act according to what you wish to convey. Remember, it's you who should be controlling your emotions, not the other way around.

And then, of course, there's always the option of not changing your style at all and bearing whatever consequences it may entail. Something along these lines happened to Esther R. Dyer, Ph.D., President and CEO of National Medical Fellowship, Inc., who was turned down for a position in government due to her communication style. "I tend to talk a lot and be very transparent. I didn't get a national job in Washington D.C. because I was very honest from the get-go and said what was on my mind. This changed the mood in the room. It wasn't what they wanted to hear. I wanted to be myself, but all in all it was a lesson learned because had I strayed away from myself and my personality, I wouldn't be where I am today, at a happy place."

Certain environments, industries, organizations or companies require communication styles that are so different from what you're willing to adjust to that it's best to reconsider your connection to them. It is perfectly valid—almost necessary—to define your boundaries. You must also determine the extent to which you are willing to go to adapt your style to different contexts and situations. In Esther's case, she decided to speak the way she normally would, and when she realized her style was not acceptable where she was interviewing, she knew it was a bad fit for her.

Arturo Poiré's Corner
✦

"We must understand what it is about passion that makes us lose control; what's behind it; what energizes that passion and makes others consider it excessive. Are we too attached to being right? To being acknowledged? Are we afraid of losing face in front of others? It's important to learn what triggers an extreme passion level in each of us."

Keys to Effective Communication

Modulating the "volume" of your emotions to effectively communicate in the workplace is not the only factor you should take into consideration. Our language and culture have specific characteristics. In my case, my mother tongue is Spanish. It requires 20%–25% more words than English to convey the same message. It contains such a wealth of grammatical flexibility that it enables greater subtleties for expression. It even allows the creation of sentences with multiple subordinate clauses. Now then, when you consider these characteristics, add your gender, and put it all into practice—especially in corporate America or global companies— you will inevitably realize some things are not optimal. You'll need to make adjustments to gain more responsibility in your field.

⬧ **Be concise.** Limit the amount of irrelevant context offered to add greater visibility to what you want to convey. If you add context, limit it to data that is an added value to your main point. For example, when describing your experiences regarding a product your department handles for which you're suggesting new solutions, be brief in your statements; especially when presenting before a group (no matter how small), and when addressing your supervisors and employees. It's best to project clear thoughts and avoid long, detailed stories. Save it for social gatherings.

⬧ **Be clear.** In many cultures expressing feelings directly and clearly doesn't come easily. People beat around the bush which results in convoluted communication that frequently leaves the audience confused. Because it's crucial for career advancement, I've advised many professional women in this particular area. Leaders should express themselves clearly and cogently. If your definition of success includes being a leader, then this step is critical for you to review.

✧ **Be straightforward.** This is a delicate subject because at times being too blunt may be perceived as being rude, aggressive or confrontational. (As was the case for Maryelena and Lina Meruane during their job interviews.) There are even certain unwritten rules in the workplace that are taken for granted and about which nothing is openly said. (You will need the guidance of mentors within your organization to learn how to best navigate them.) It is of paramount importance to find a happy medium to express yourself clearly and concisely. Women tend not to communicate what they want directly, assuming that if others are paying attention, they should guess it. Then there are Latinas like Maryelena who are at the opposite end of this spectrum. And others, like Lina Meruane, who, when under stress, revert automatically to their native communication style instead of exercising the required level of subtlety to articulate their thoughts adequately.

The challenge comes in striking a balance. To achieve it, it helps to ask your advisory team for feedback.

THE VOICE OF EXPERIENCE

"When I was promoted to manager I was surprised to know that I was the only one out of fifteen managers to be a female, Latina, and younger than thirty. The majority of managers were forty-five-year-old males. This experience taught me to know the male mindset in the managerial world. I learned how to speak the business "language," cut to the chase, and not fear men if they raised their voice. I matured professionally in that stage in my career because I was able to interact daily with people who were very different from me and managed to develop a nice professional friendship with the group."

—*Anna Giraldo-Kerr, Founder and President of Shades of Success Coaching Inc.*

✧ **Speak English well.** If you work in the U.S. or for a multinational company abroad, you should perfect your English. I was lucky to have studied English in Argentina when I was young so that I could arrive to this country with a high level of fluency. Over time I significantly improved my skills. But this is not the case for many professional foreigners who live in the U.S. Although it's much harder to learn a language when you're an adult, it's not impossible. The truth is that leaders are expected to excel at English. Unfortunately, people tend to equate an inability to communicate in English with lack of smarts; therefore, for the benefit of your advancement, it is critical not to fall into that trap.

✧ **Accepting (or not accepting) your accent.** Having an accent may become an issue if it impedes others from understanding you. If you learned English later in life, it's very likely that you have an accent which will be almost impossible to get rid of. I like my accent and I never intended to get rid of it because it differentiates me from the rest. As with other things in life, I chose to view my accent as an opportunity to distinguish myself and not an inhibitor. If you have an accent, you probably have the same experience I do when I meet someone. The first thing someone will say is, "hello," and the second thing is, "where are you from?" I know people who get offended when they're asked this question, as if they were being excluded or considered second class citizens, undesirable immigrants or who knows what. That's the story they choose to believe using their own filters which reveal old insecurities and complexes. I prefer to choose a story about curiosity, and how my accent may enable a stranger to strike up a conversation with me because they feel I'm approachable (a plus in all relationships). Now, if your accent is excessively dense and makes understanding what you're saying difficult, then it's time to take a few courses on accent reduction to improve your comprehensibility. Instead of thinking this implies changing who you are, consider that your priority is carrying out actions that align to your dreams and to what brings you satisfaction. If you are to move toward those goals, you must be able to convey your knowledge and ideas in order to project the image you strive for. This way others will understand you, feel inspired by you, value your contributions, and follow you.

But an accent is not just an immigrant/nonimmigrant marker but also a marker of your country of origin, social class, and region. You'll notice that the majority of top executives have a similar accent which typically belongs to the Northeast of the U.S. In New York, the Upper East Side accent denotes a higher social status than a Bronx one. And you may have noticed that a British accent is considered higher on the hierarchy than an American one. (It is well known that Americans tend to grant immediate credibility to a British person.) Almost unconsciously an accent functions as a marker for inclusion or exclusion. We all rely on accents to identify members of our group (or tribe) and we tend to gravitate toward those that are similar to ours.

Depending on the environment and industry you work in and the hierarchical level you'd like to reach, it will be more or less important to polish your accent and expressions to gain access. But I wouldn't become obsessed with the accent unless it's holding you back from being understood. It's simply good to be aware that it's there and that it's just another marker by which people build stories about you as you build yours about others.

✧ **Practice your *sound bites.*** This media term is used to describe short clips of speech taken from a longer piece of audio. It's usually a pithy phrase or sentence that embodies the speaker's main point. Thanks to the numerous media segments I've done over the years, I've been able to perfect my communication style. When you're given just two to four minutes to summarize valuable information that could fill an entire book, you're forced to set aside what's superfluous to bring out what's relevant. This provides conciseness and clarity. And it's a great way of taking a complex idea, processing it, and "digesting it" so that your audience can quickly understand it. Below are six strategic steps for turning your ideas into sound bites.

How to Transform a Complex Thought into a "Digestible" Idea

- **Step 1:** The first thing I do is choose the topic I'll be talking about. (I'm often the one who proposes the subject on programs I participate in.) Let's assume the topic is: Take advantage of your female traits to reap professional benefits.
- **Step 2:** I think of three or four points I'd like to highlight about this topic.
- **Step 3:** I write up short explanatory paragraphs for each point.
- **Step 4:** I say each point out loud (yes, real nutty!), its explanation and rephrase what doesn't sound right.
- **Step 5:** I read my sound bites aloud and take my time.
- **Step 6:** I practice articulating each concept several times without reading until I feel I can spontaneously answer each of the interviewer's questions.

Obviously, at work where you're asked questions throughout the day, it's impossible to practice all the answers. I'm proposing you test my strategy when you need to express your opinion at a team meeting, when requesting a salary increase, when attending a meeting with a new client you'll be offering your services to, or when you wish to explain a decision to your employees. These are all examples of occasions where you could put into practice a clear and concise communication style.

Many believe they don't have to prepare themselves because words come easy to them. This is a great conceptual mistake for two reasons. First, like everything in life, practice makes perfect. Even people who are born with unique talents must constantly prepare themselves if they want to grow their careers. Take great musicians for example, and the numerous hours a day they spend practicing the piano or the violin. And scientists; How many years do they spend locked up in their labs testing and retesting minimum variations on their experiments until they finally hit the nail on that discovery they were after for so long? Second, when you're under great stress—as in a salary negotiation—one's emotions are involved as well. Emotions inevitably impact your communication style. When you practice what you want to say your brain stores that information and accesses it when required. This way, it's harder for your emotions to get in the way at critical times.

What's interesting is that the brain doesn't distinguish between mental and physical rehearsal. That's why elite athletes use a technique called *mental rehearsal* before a race, fight or other sports event. They sit down and mentally rehearse every small movement during the competition in order to improve their performance. For our brain, this exercise is equal to training at the gym. Imagine the impact this type of practice can have on your professional performance.

We owe the same level of dedication to our own dream. That's why we must prepare, fine-tune our tools (this includes our communication style), test new things, consult with others who are more knowledgeable, and continue studying.

Arturo Poiré's Corner
✦

"When operating at a senior executive level you must be more efficient in your communication style; it must be brief, short, concise, and straightforward. Latinas must beware because here's where many stereotype traits crop up. When meeting a top executive you must have a clear picture of what you want from him/her. Are you talking to him/her because you need his/her help? Does it involve decision-making? Do you need some feedback on some specific issue? Are you presenting a FYI report?

If you're an executive and planning to converse with your CEO or CFO, I suggest you speak in terms of "we." You already hold that position and have official recognition and it's understood that you lead your team, so their successes are your successes. At this level, successes are always shared with your team but *you* will be held responsible for the mistakes."

Never Stop Participating
A while ago I attended a talk of two leading figures in the U.S., Dr. Isabel, a psychologist who runs a program on Univision Radio and Mayte Prida, host of several television programs, and an advocate for breast cancer awareness. The presentation took place at the Spanish-language book fair, LéaLA, in Los Angeles and was aimed at women. In fact, 80% of the audience was female. Yet,

when the Q & A session took place, guess who raised their hands? Right. Those three or four men among hundreds of women. This phenomenon is observable in diverse environments, from middle school math classes to business meetings and industry conferences.

Men tend to toss their opinion because they believe that everything they have to say is important and deserves being shared. They don't need to be a hundred percent sure of the subject they're giving their opinion on. On the other hand, women tend to be more cautious and don't give their opinion until they've written a doctoral thesis on the topic. I know I'm exaggerating but not that much! Now, I ask you, if nobody knows about your opinions, ideas, suggestions, who will give you a chance? If you're afraid of speaking in public, of coming across as silly, of saying something inappropriate or of someone feeling offended, go back to the first chapters where we dealt with fears. The bottom line is that if you want to grow in your career, sooner or later you'll have to face the need to increase your visibility.

There are strategies you can implement to help make your valuable voice heard and minimize risks when "raising your hand" and becoming visible to the world.

> If you'll be proposing something controversial, be sure to get the buy-in from your boss and key members of your team before the meeting.
> If you'll be sharing something that requires analytical support, confirm the numbers before your presentation.
> If you'll be talking about something that's emotionally touching or that you feel passionate about, take a deep breath and remember that you're not sharing your idea as *the* truth. When you avoid believing you own the truth and that you're right, you also avoid making others

feel they're wrong which makes everyone uncomfortable. Explain your concern rationally and use your passion skillfully. Well-managed passion is very compelling.

➤ Try listening to your voice as you speak and be aware of when it becomes more high-pitched. This typically happens when you're enthused; you get angry, or emotional and therefore your message is harder to understand. To lower your pitch, breathe naturally and deeply from your diaphragm.

➤ By all means avoid criticizing your boss in public. Say whatever you have to say to your boss privately so as not to challenge their authority in front of the group.

THE VOICE OF EXPERIENCE

"When somebody listens to you it's as if that person sees the way you're dressed and how you think—this woman is rich, or poor, educated, cool, a nerd, wants to seduce me or is unpleasant. You generate responses; you may control some but not others because these depend on the listener. Paul Watzlawick, a communication theorist, argues that it's impossible not to communicate; our body is full of messages and language, even silence; language is always performative. It's useful to understand this if we're seeking a successful exchange. This means we must know how to adjust our performance to the expectations of the person we're addressing. So, if you wear jeans to a job interview, that says to the interviewer, 'I don't respect your work; I'm taking it lightly.'"

—*Lina Meruane, Literature Professor at NewYorkUniveristy*

Chapter 7

The Art of Negotiating

Famous Women Speak: Ambassador Ivonne Baki

Ivonne Baki is an Ecuadorian-Lebanese politician with global influence. Ivonne has been involved in intergovernmental and international peace talks for several decades as Ecuador's Industry Minister, President of the Commission of the Andean Community of Nations, Ecuadorian Ambassador to the U.S. and Lebanon, and as UNESCO's Goodwill Ambassador, among many other key positions. Since 2010 she's served as head of Ecuador's Yasuní-ITT initiative, a project for the conservation of the largest biodiversity area on our planet located in an oil zone.

Q: *With a master's degree in public administration from Harvard, you started your negotiation career as a member of the board of directors of a nonprofit organization called Conflict Management Group. What drew you to work in this sector typically not populated by women?*

A: That was precisely the reason. The fact that I didn't see women in peace negotiations, especially between countries with issues such as Israel and Palestine, Ecuador and Peru. I lived through the Lebanese war. My children were born under the bombs; I saw what violence entails and I was never able to understand why people kill in the name of religion. Something had to be done in the name of peace and it

107

wasn't being done. At the negotiation table there were always men who saw their own position but never the common interest. That's the difference between men and women. Women see common interest and try to find a joint solution, whereas men say, "This is what I want and I won't budge." The truth is that you must always see both sides to reach a win-win position; you win a little and the other side wins a little too and you thus reach an agreement. At the beginning I didn't know that. I started painting and through art I expressed what I thought about peace, until I was invited to Harvard University as a resident artist. I then went to Harvard Kennedy School for a master's program in public administration because I thought that as an artist I wouldn't be able to make a difference in the peace issue. That's where I met Roger Fisher, the negotiation guru, and he was my mentor. When I finished my master's program I got involved in conflict resolution and began to negotiate in different regions including the Middle East where no solution has been found yet. We conducted a three-year negotiation between Ecuador and Peru. That was a unique experience. And that's how I started my career in politics and negotiation.

Q: *Which were a few of your major challenges during your diplomatic career as a Latina/Arab woman in the U.S., Lebanon, and Ecuador? Did you notice any difference in how you were treated as a woman in each of these countries?*

A: Let me share a story so you can realize how things were when I started. When I arrived in Washington as ambassador, I was one of three women ambassadors out of all the 193 countries. A few years later the book *And Then There Were Ten* was published because we eventually grew to ten women. We were interviewed a lot since it was the first time we reached that number. As ambassador, I was invited to a cocktail—I believe at the Lebanese Embassy—attended by all Arab ambassadors. When I was introduced to the Egyptian ambassador, the host said, "She's the Ecuadorian ambassador to Washington." Do you know what the Egyptian ambassador asked me? He said, "And where is your husband, the ambassador?" We later became good friends, but this was just to give you an idea of a woman's role in the year 1998.

Q: *We owe you our gratitude for several important cooperation treaties signed between Latin American countries. What are some of your secret weapons when negotiating?*

A: I don't believe there are secret weapons. I believe the secret lies in knowing the art of negotiation; the art of stepping into the other person's shoes. You can't start a negotiation if you don't know who you're facing. The truth is, you shouldn't be seated opposite the other party but side-by-side. It's a serious mistake often made to sit at the table in front of your opponent. The best way is to have the person sit beside you, you may even have to touch the person when necessary, and step into his/her shoes.

Q: *What made you get involved in the Yasuní-ITT negotiations to preserve the biodiversity in Educador's Yasuni Park?*

A: Two things have changed my life: the Lebanese war and visiting this magic place. I thought Galapagos was the most magical place on Earth until I discovered Yasuni Park. When you visit it you find yourself in the middle of nature; the connection of the earth with God and humanity. There's a great variety of plants and animals and there are two communities living in voluntary isolation, the last two on the whole planet. Communities from this region enjoy millenary wisdom; they have plants and poisons to cure all types of diseases. But the region also has another type of wealth: oil. Ecuador still depends on oil exports and 20% of the country's oil is located in that area. When you visit it you realize it's a sacred place and we must take care of it for the sake of humanity. Negotiations are not easy; we must campaign a lot because nobody knows the place or the situation at hand.

Q: *How do you manage to be a mother and lead such an active life, always on a plane with homes in Lebanon, Ecuador, and the U.S.? How do you strike a balance?*

A: True. Sometimes I wonder how I do it because I'm a mother, wife, and grandmother. But I'm always in touch with my husband and children. Being there physically is not what's most important. I got used to the lifestyle and my bag is always ready. Traveling to me is the only moment I can relax and have some time to myself; I can write and think without interruptions. At the same time, I feel at home everywhere. The same holds true when I speak another language; I only think in that language. That's what it means to be a citizen of the world. That's what we all are right now, citizens of the world. Where you're at no longer makes a difference.

You can access the complete interview with Ivonne Baki here: http://www.youtube.com/watch?v=TXQRqZCOj-w.

In her book *The Female Brand: Using the Female Mindset to Succeed in Business* (Davies-Black, 2009), Catherine Kaputa shares a story about a woman whose job was to supervise hundreds of employees for a Wall Street company. Several months before annual performance evaluations took place male employees would approach her office to negotiate their bonuses. They presented their case and even made it clear how much of a bonus they expected to get. In contrast, not one female did that type of lobbying, which is a mistake. This is what happens (and not just in Wall Street) when managers do the math to distribute monies: they keep in mind how much each one asked for and consider *if I don't give John a figure that's close to what he asked for he might quit.* During this process, these same managers—it doesn't really matter whether they're male or female—think *Jane didn't ask for anything so maybe I can save myself some money and give her a smaller share.*

THE VOICE OF EXPERIENCE

"One way or another you negotiate every single day. People fear the word negotiation but, in truth, it's only a question of positioning your argument to get to *yes*. Negotiating is also trying to reach consensus with your team. People forget that negotiating is not just closing some formal deal but also what we do every single day of our lives."

—*Laureen Ong, President of Travel Channel Media*

This setting is replicated in all industries and starts very early on in women's careers. Or rather, it starts very early on in women's lives when we get used to not asking for anything, imagining we'll be given what we deserve, or assuming that if we do our job well, we'll be appreciated.

According to studies, part of the reason why women don't negotiate is because they're convinced their circumstances are fixed and out of their control, whereas men tend to see negotiation possibilities everywhere. Likewise, the sense of entitlement is weaker in females than in men. A study on this topic was conducted by psychologists Charlene Callahan-Levy and Lawrence Messe[1] whereby they recruited students to write their opinions on college-related subjects. Then they were asked to decide how much they would pay themselves and how much they would pay a third party to do that work. Researchers found out that females would pay themselves for that task 19% less than males would.

Another study asked MBA students to negotiate a hypothetical job with a real-life recruiter. The researcher interviewed students and asked them whether they thought they were entitled to receive an equal or better salary than the one the recruiter was offering other candidates. Out of the students who said they were entitled to more, 70% were male, and out of those who considered

---

1. *Sex differences in the allocation of pay*, Callahan-Levy, C.M and L.A. Messe. Journal of Personality and Social Psychology, 37(3):433–446, 1979.

they were entitled to the same salary, 71% were female. I believe that for women, a sense of fairness and a need to follow rules often comes into play in these situations. As we've seen, it's likely these behavioral traits were instilled early on in childhood through games and during interactions with adults in their lives.

THE VOICE OF EXPERIENCE

"Typically, negotiating power lies in being objective, and also in numbers. When I used to negotiate multimillion dollar contracts at Johnson & Johnson, I always took my time to create Excel models that enabled me to forecast scenarios and figures to have real-time answers available. These spreadsheets were my secret weapon at the negotiation table because I was able to see right there and then that some of the things being suggested at the meeting wouldn't work."

—Liliana Gil, cofounder and managing partner at XL Alliance

Other studies[2] show that out of those MBA students who graduated from Ivy League universities, males who negotiated their salaries received a 4.3% increase vis-à-vis the initial offer whereas females were only able to increase that offer by 2.7%. Which means that already by the initial salary offer males obtained 59% more money than females. Consider this, if males continue to negotiate 59% more than females every chance they get throughout their careers, by the time they retire they'll have earned a lot more money than us.

Females in the U.S. currently earn, on average, 77% of what males earn. This male-female wage gap varies in different groups. For example, Latinas earn 89.5% of what Latinos earn. According

2. "Gender differences in current and starting salaries: The role of performance, college major, and job title," Gerhart, B. *Industrial and Labor Relations Review* 43(4) 418–433, 1990.

to Catalyst,[3] a well-known organization interested in promoting female equality in the workplace, Latinas earn 60% of what a white male earns, and 53% of what Asians earn (the best paid of all groups). Numerous theories attempt to explain the reasons for such a disparity. Some studies suggest that the gap can be explained on a division of labor. Women are more likely than men to have interrupted careers to raise a family, taking time off for child care or elder care, and are more likely to work part-time. Further studies show that more women tend to be employed in support occupations, positions that are paid less than other professions. Meanwhile, Catalyst research has found that a significant wage gap still exists even when factors such as the number of years of prior experience, professional level, industry, region, etc., were considered, all of which points toward systemic discrimination.

THE VOICE OF EXPERIENCE

"The business culture has a special way of thinking that says it's not worth investing in women's careers because sooner or later they'll get married and have children. According to my professional experience as an executive and businesswoman I notice the lack of labor equality in two areas, both in positions and wages. Women have traditionally been assigned jobs where organizing and care giving are the main tasks. In contrast, men are assigned jobs where decision-making and negotiating agreements are key. Over time, this difference has created obstacles that contribute to endemic labor inequality. It has nourished the inner belief in men and women that women's capacity is limited. And it has created a business culture with rules, policies, and regulations that reward male over female roles."

—Anna Giraldo-Kerr, Founder and President of
Shades for Success Coaching Inc.

---

3. "Women's Earnings and Income," *Catalyst*, April 2011.

The male-female income gap can also be attributed to the lack of self-confidence a great deal of women experience. This can lead to not expressing their opinion at meetings, not arguing when they disagree, and performing jobs with little visibility that are valued by few. There's also this deep-rooted belief that women don't deserve to earn more than what is being offered to them and that you don't have to negotiate but rather accept what is given. Just as María Marín, author of the book *Ask More, Expect More and You'll Get More* (Aguilar, 2010), says, "We don't have what we want simply because we don't dare ask for it. There's a saying in negotiation that goes, 'In business as in life you don't get what you deserve, you get what you negotiate.' So you can't be afraid of asking more and demanding more."

Sometimes, the reason why women earn less is because they don't know how much other people with similar responsibilities are earning both in their company and in the industry. Men tend to share this data more freely whereas women don't ask. As Catherine McKenzie, Senior Producer for ABC's "Good Morning America" says, "If you work in the private sector and your parents and friends don't work in corporations, how do you find out how much you're worth or what additional benefits you can ask for? How do you find out in your industry that you're entitled to a car to go back and forth, or more vacation time instead of extra money?"

This is why I increasingly tap into my close network of colleagues (male and female) for guidance on how much to charge for different types of presentations or activities I'm asked to do. By doing so I find out what they've charged and what baseline fee I should negotiate from. I also think it is significant for our growth as women to share this information with other women who are less advanced in their careers than us.

For example, I recently met a young lady at a conference who had just launched her online platform and was enthused about partnering with a big media platform. I looked into it a little bit and found out she wasn't going to be paid for the content she would provide the big media platform in exchange for a link to her site. And although this sounds great when getting started, you soon realize it's much more costly for you to produce content than it is for them to redirect traffic to your site. I advised her on how to handle the situation so as not to sign a disadvantageous agreement, something I wasn't told myself before entering into a similar agreement some time back. Until you get used to having these conversations with friends and colleagues, here are some sites you can visit to compare wage data within the U.S.: www.glassdoor.com, www.payscale.com, www.vault.com and www.salary.com.

This aversion towards negotiation places women at a disadvantage in more ways than financially. We aren't negotiating the type of responsibilities assigned to us or the budgets we need to carry out a project with either. Anna Giraldo-Kerr explains that this passive attitude, this silence, is interpreted as a lack of knowledge and trust in yourself. And as a result, women will continue to access less visible jobs and receive less salary. As business owners this "allergy" towards negotiating impacts us even further because no one other than you is responsible for your income and company's survival. It's always good to have a group of business advisors as offered by the Small Business Administration in the U.S. (www.sba.gov), as well as by your local chamber of commerce.

Before moving on I'd like to be very clear on this point: the only person responsible for your career development is *you*. If you don't ask for what you need, if you don't talk about your achievements, if you don't negotiate your promotions at every step, as well as your projects and responsibilities, nobody will do it for you. If you don't establish clear goals, it'll be easier for others to pull you toward areas that won't benefit or satisfy you. Be sure to sit in the driver's seat of your career at all times.

THE VOICE OF EXPERIENCE

"Every role in my life has been a negotiation. I negotiated with my employer to pay 100% of my MBA program. I also had to negotiate striking a balance between home and work. And being a good negotiator led to handling vendors successfully. I was responsible not only for negotiating contracts, but also final product and services."
—*Carla Dodd, Senior Director Multicultural Marketing for Walmart Stores*

How to Get Started

As several women I interviewed pointed out, you spend your life negotiating although you may not realize that "that" is negotiating. So it's best to begin by identifying what situations are negotiable. You'll be surprised to hear that any given situation where someone wants something may be subject to negotiation. Whether you want something and need another's cooperation or others want something and you may be (or may position yourself as) the means for them to achieve it. This also includes buying and selling scenarios, regardless of who's the buyer, who's the seller, and what product or service is being traded. All situations both personal and in the workplace have the potential to be negotiated. Here are some examples of negotiation in the workplace:

> The location of your desk or office
> The amount of days you work from home
> Your job title
> What percentage of your master's program will be paid by the company

> ➤ What foreign country you'll be transferred to on your next promotion

And these are some examples from your family life:

> ➤ When it's your turn to cook during the week
> ➤ Who picks up the kids from daycare after work
> ➤ How many hours a day your teenagers may use the computer other than for academic purposes

You see, the list is endless because the truth is, in life, almost everything is subject to negotiation. Perhaps once you realize how permeated daily life is with small negotiations, and how successful you are at some of them, you can shake off the bias and face those career negotiations more naturally.

Arturo Poiré's Corner
✦

"If you don't show you are sure of yourself and express your needs, plans, etc., negotiating can be very hard. That is, we go back to "expecting acknowledgement" which, generally speaking, is what women tend to do. In any negotiation the person who is able to convey self-confidence, conviction of ideas, and certainty that what's being asked for is well deserved, has an advantage. Another aspect impacting women is handling emotions. The best negotiators are able to control their emotions, appear rational and never take anything personally. Many women, however, cry when they're furious or frustrated as a biological reaction that's hard to control. My suggestion is not to pile up your frustration without articulating it because you end up bursting. Secondly, if you shed tears at a meeting because you're angry, you should be able to explain what's happening. I've seen many women do this and it proves effective for people to understand she's not crying out of weakness but because she's angry or frustrated."

Finding Your Own Style

The first thing I'd like to highlight is that you must find your individual negotiation style as you're pursuing your own definition of success. And although I'm offering you some negotiation pointers in this chapter, nothing will make sense if you try to copy someone else's style or use these tools without conviction. As Carla Dodds from Walmart U.S. says, "I was hired at Walmart for my negotiating skills. I've negotiated billion dollar contracts. When training women in my team I used to tell them, 'Don't try to negotiate like me. I'll give you the basic elements so that you know the keys to a good negotiation, but once you feel at ease you'll find your own voice and nobody will beat you at it.'"

Just like copying a man's style isn't a smart strategy, it's also not a good idea to imitate another woman whose own style works for her, but may not be the best for you.

The Winning Strategy

When negotiating professionally, I suggest you keep in mind the following steps to obtain optimal results in your negotiations.

First, decide what you want. Set a clear goal. For instance, if you're negotiating a new job, decide beforehand how much the acceptable salary floor will be considering your expertise, wage history, how much the industry pays for your skill set, how much that particular company pays, and the market supply/demand situation at the historical moment you're in. In the example we'll be working on, let's say your asking salary is $100,000 and the least you'll accept is $75,000. Decide what benefits you'd like to receive. Make a list of everything you want and prioritize those items. For example, a flexible schedule, an administrative assistant, a car, a corporate credit card, and five weeks paid vacation time. Although this example is about negotiating a new job position, use these same steps if you want to negotiate a contract for your own company.

THE VOICE OF EXPERIENCE

"You must always talk about your value proposition: 'Look, here's what I think, here's what I want, here's what I think is beneficial for the company, and here's why I think it would be beneficial for me.'"
—*Gloria Ysasi-Díaz, Vice President, Supply Chain at Grainger*

Second, step into the shoes of the person you're negotiating with since there's no better strategy than the *win-win* strategy where both parties have something to gain. According to Gloria Puentes, National Director of UPMC's Dignity and Respect Campaign, "Being a good negotiator doesn't necessarily mean you get to close a deal every single time, but that you win over time. To me, being a good negotiator means finding common ground; all parties must win."

Ask yourself, how does the other party want to benefit from this negotiation or what benefit do they want to reap from it? How can I present my proposal considering the needs of all parties involved? In order for this strategy to be successful you must know as much as possible about the other party's situation before the negotiation takes place. Getting to know their goals, who they want to impress, what challenges they face, the political climate within the company, and other details about their situation will provide tools for you to later present an appealing plan. In this example, let's say the position has been open for some time now; they need someone with your skills, knowledge, and expertise who could start right away because they've just launched a new division and need a unit leader.

THE VOICE OF EXPERIENCE

"In order to negotiate in the Armed Forces I would do the research as if I were a lawyer. It was critical to prepare for whatever they might ask because that's the best way to negotiate. Not to approach the subject emotionally, but rather bring the facts to the table. Saying 'because I want this' is not enough. You must anticipate questions and see things from the other party's perspective."

—*Cristina Vilella, retired Lieutenant Colonel of the U.S. Air Force*

Third, decide what you're willing to give up in the negotiation. For example, the possibility of working from home and having an assistant are two nonnegotiable items but you could live without the credit card and without the car.

Fourth, you must decide what your minimum salary requirement is; the point where you'll say no to the offer and walk away from the negotiation table (or quit your job if you're negotiating a wage increase) because it doesn't meet the minimum requirement you established before starting the negotiation. If you haven't set clear priorities, i.e., the elements you're willing to give up and the ones you're not, you won't have enough flexibility to negotiate. And without first establishing a bottom line (the absolute lowest you'll go) below which you won't accept the job, you'll lack a strong enough position to negotiate everything that you could with your potential employer. People know very well when you're negotiating from a strong position and measure how much they can push knowing that if they don't come close to your minimum they're bound to lose you.

Fifth, you must ask yourself what you want. If you prepare your thoughts and never get to the point of actually asking what you want, chances are nobody will guess what it is. If you're asking for a raise, prepare a list of your achievements and how these have impacted the company's bottom line. Submit the list to your boss before the meeting to discuss your compensation. Then, gather all the necessary information to bring to the meeting and the objective elements to support your request (for instance, how much others earn in similar positions with equal skills, the company's financial situation, etc.). Practice what you'll say so that your presentation sounds rational and include pointers that will interest your boss and the company. Don't base your arguments on "I deserve this raise because I've been working for the company for five years."

You can use this strategy to negotiate almost anything. Whenever you identify the needs of the parties involved, know the competitors' and market's situation, and present proposals that take all these factors into consideration, you're substantially increasing your chances of walking out with a better deal.

THE VOICE OF EXPERIENCE

"In a negotiation it is important for both parties to save face. In the U.S. we talk a lot about this when doing business with Asians, but we don't realize that here, too, people must save face. Everybody has an ego and when negotiating you must try to give other parties a way out without embarrassing them. They mustn't feel they've given it all up and received nothing in exchange, or that they've reached an agreement which ultimately hurts them."

—*Susan Landon, Executive Recruiter for DHR International*

What Happens When You Don't Get What You're Looking For?

When negotiations fail and you don't reach an agreement, one of the parties (in this case you) may consider an alternative: the Best Alternative to a Negotiated Agreement or BATNA.[4] It's important not to confuse your BATNA with the minimum required wage you established which, if not met, would ultimately be the reason to walk away from the negotiation. Having a bottom line means "in the worst case scenario I'll take this."

The purpose of a BATNA is to determine a course of action if the agreement is not reached within a certain time frame. Having a BATNA enables greater flexibility and creativity than when you just establish a minimum salary requirement. The idea is not to begin negotiations putting your BATNA on the table. You should have it prepared in case things don't work out the way you wanted them to.

In order to understand this notion you must acknowledge that when you negotiate several factors come into play that go beyond what you're negotiating at that very moment. These factors are often hard to assess quantitatively, but in the earlier example, for instance, where you're negotiating a job offer, it's not just your salary that is at stake. Other factors such as your relationship with the parties involved, trusting the other party in fulfilling the agreement, the value of the time and efforts made in the negotiation process, etc., must also be considered.

Let's Now See an Example of BATNA in Action

You receive a job offer from Acme Company for $100,000. When you interview with other employers your BATNA is $100,000 be-

4. The concept of BATNA was developed by Roger Fisher and William Ury's Harvard Negotiation Project in their book *Getting to Yes*.

cause you already have this offer at hand without having to negotiate with another company. Now, examine the following alternatives:

> You get an $85,000 job offer from a company that's in your same neighborhood which will allow for a short and less-costly commute as well as the ability to arrive home at a decent hour to enjoy your family.
> You get a $60,000 basic salary offer plus an annual bonus which may hypothetically add an extra $60,000.
> You get a $90,000 offer from someone you've known for years and have a close relationship with.

YOUR VOICE THROUGH SOCIAL NETWORKS

"In a negotiation you must never take things personally. If you feel you might lose a point, give in a little and you might receive something else unexpectedly."
—*Miriam Fabiancic, former Editor in Chief of Mosaico Book Club, via Facebook*

In preparing your BATNA, you might leverage two advantageous traits often seen in people born into Latino families: the ability to think creatively and out of the box, and the ability to solve problems. Therefore:

> Ask a friend or colleague to help you think about all the alternatives you would consider if the negotiation fails.
> Choose the most promising alternatives and develop them to see if they'll work.
> Identify the best alternative and keep it handy in case you need to use it as a second option during the negotiation process.

Let's continue with the earlier example. During conversations with Acme you were offered $100,000 and were told they couldn't give you the car or credit card. They can't provide you with an assistant either. You're thinking Acme might not be your best option because they don't seem ready to give you what you want. Before your last meeting with them you've looked into all other offers and decided to present the following alternative (your BATNA): a $100,000 salary for a four-day workweek from 9:00 AM to 7:00 PM, a five-week vacation, freedom to hire interns at your discretion, and a better job title than initially offered.

If you want to grow in your career, consider a strategy men often use: quitting their jobs and moving to a position with greater responsibility and a better salary elsewhere. Though women don't always seem to feel as free as men to do this, it's a strategy worth considering.

THE VOICE OF EXPERIENCE

"Women stay on too long in companies waiting to be appreciated and promoted. Years back when I used to whine about not being appreciated at my job and not getting the promotions I deserved, a friend of mine said to me, 'You must respect yourself. Go elsewhere!' If you know the industry, go look for another company where you'll be appreciated more. Many years ago, a lady once told me that the majority of promotions she attained at work weren't because of the great job she did but because she had an offer somewhere else. For us women this concept is hard to grasp because we experience it as if we were deceiving our boyfriend. But it is critical that you establish a contact network in your industry and industries akin to yours where your skills may be applicable."

—*Catherine McKenzie, Senior Producer at ABC's*
"Good Morning America"

Be True to Yourself

When examining the results men obtain from their negotiation skills it's tempting to want to copy their style. As Mika Brzezinski points out in her book *Knowing Your Value* (Weinstein Books, 2010), many men (including Joe Scarborough, her cohost on MSNBC's "Morning Joe" program) raise their voice, curse, point an accusing finger at their bosses, threaten to quit, and, a few minutes later, after getting what they want, end up talking about sports and drinking beer together.

The problem the majority of us women face is that we feel uncomfortable acting in such a manner due to how we were raised. Most of us were trained to be good and complacent girls; we were taught not to fight, raise our voice or curse. How many times did your mom tell you not to use four-letter words? These messages are so deeply rooted that we don't realize they're part of the filter through which we approach negotiating. These beliefs are so inscribed in our conscience that we simply say, "I don't know how to negotiate" or "that's not me." But if you can deconstruct this message, as you've practiced at the beginning of the book, you'll realize that you're capable of stating a new reality for yourself. And one that insists, "I'm an excellent negotiator."

- -

THE VOICE OF EXPERIENCE

"To me, the best negotiation strategy is being ready to get up and walk away from the table. Knowing your limitations and sticking to them. There have been times when I was too desperate and I accepted less than I really wanted. I felt strong only when I was able to walk away from the table because the deal wasn't beneficial to me. I was afraid, true, but I was proud of having stood up for my own interests. Once you've done it the first time, it's easier the second time around. You must keep in mind that not accepting a negotiation is not the end of the world. There will always be another one."

—*Christine LeViseur Mendonça, Managing Director for Shore to Shore Advisory, LLC, and Operations Director of Latinos in College*

Studies show that the aggressive attitude sometimes displayed by men generates a negative perception if exhibited by our gender. When a man acts this way he's considered temperamental; he knows what he wants and he's a good negotiator. Conversely, a woman is judged as crazy, a bitch or it must be "that time of the month." It may seem impossible to win this battle, but it's not.

The secret lies in knowing your worth, keeping your integrity, being true to yourself, and creating alliances with men who could support you throughout the negotiation process. If you aren't offered the minimum requirements you set for yourself as part of the deal, be willing to walk away from the offer. If cursing is not in tune with your personality, don't do it. And if you're not the type to threaten your bosses with quitting, avoid getting into that situation. The idea is to adapt a forward-thinking mindset that's beneficial to achieving your goals without setting aside who you are or negatively impacting your image. Therefore, if you need to learn how to negotiate and ask for what you want, use the resources provided in this chapter and seek additional help to learn how. Don't simply try to imitate what men in your environment do without considering what's at stake when implementing such a change in attitude.

YOUR VOICE THROUGH SOCIAL NETWORKS

"Truthfully, in the business world everything revolves around money. So women must sharpen their financial knowledge

> and make sure that income and profitability are key compo-
> nents in their employment performance. Develop them, use
> them and learn how to market your skills to bring income in-
> to your company. To all of the above add negotiation skills.
> The more money you bring in through negotiations, the more
> people will seek you as a member of their teams."
> —*Midy Aponte, Founder and CEO of the consulting*
> *agency Sánchez Ricardo, via Facebook*

I'd like to finish this chapter with what Daisy Auger-Domínguez from Disney said to me when I asked her what role being a good negotiator had played in her career success: "This reminds me of a great Martin Luther King Jr. quote, 'A genuine leader is not a searcher of consensus but a molder of consensus.' One of my greatest achievements has been to combine my knowledge and experiences into a format that allows me to emerge as an effective negotiator. I do this by carefully and sensitively navigating the channels of competing interests and diverse stakeholders, genuinely partnering with colleagues and critical stakeholders, formulating well-balanced and comprehensive strategic initiatives, and delivering great results. This is a skill I hone on an everyday basis and which forms the foundation for my professional achievements."

I believe all of us can use a good dose of Daisy's attitude when negotiating.

Chapter 8

How to Create a Positive Impression

on Your Bosses

Famous Women Speak: Nancy Dubuc

Since being promoted to the top job at Lifetime Networks in 2010 Nancy Dubuc has focused on reinventing the brand, something she's currently doing for the History channel which was recently added to her portfolio of responsibilities. She's launched successful series such as "The Hatfields and McCoys," "Pawn Stars," "Army Wives," "The Client List," "Dance Moms," and is now focusing on developing scripted series and movies for Lifetime Movie Network. But success is nothing new for Nancy, who's rose through the ranks and in her own words, "worked her ass off" to get here.

Q: *How did you get to your current position?*
A: I really got here by putting one foot in front of the other and by doing what I always recommend to people, "pick the boss, not the job." In the end, you will be shaped by a boss, a peer, a mentor. It is your responsibility to find these people.

Q: *Why do you think you made it?*
A: I think this year, for the first time, I can say that I'm a good leader. Up

until recently, I didn't have the opportunities to chart my own course but now I do and that's great. You know, women don't talk enough about power. But power is good. We talk about how hard it is to be the number two or three in an organization. But once you sit in that chair, things are easier. You get to make the decisions and of course, with big power comes big accountability, and that's fine.

Q: *Along the way you've remained real and approachable which has probably helped you stay in touch with your audience. I also get the sense that you are someone with a lot of common sense, something that's not that easy to find.*

A: Yes, I don't know why it's so hard. I like to stay close to the process, and even do something that drives my assistant crazy. Once a month I'll take a meeting with someone who has cold called me. It could be a student, it could be a woman, it could be anyone. I never know because I just pick one request randomly.

Q: *Is there something that you particularly dislike about your high power position?*

A: Nothing frustrates me more than the fact that I get all the credit for things that my team does. It makes me bonkers. The truth is that I have a loyal, fearless group of executives who are my inner circle. My biggest satisfaction comes from watching a team epically dysfunctional, become highly functional. It's a journey.

Perhaps one of the greatest challenges women face today as they grow professionally is creating a positive impression on the senior staff within their organizations. Even more so in today's job world where you might have to report to several individuals, some of which may not even be in the same physical location you're in. I'll let Arturo Poiré introduce the topic we'll be discussing in this chapter so we can kick off the conversation.

Arturo Poiré's Corner
✦

"The idea of creating a positive image with our superiors underpins the notion that they need and value different things than our peers and junior associates do. This is true. They not only value different things, but give special importance to your skills and behavior. Which are the traits most valued by senior employers? Being responsible, having a sense of urgency, being reliable, having good judgment to prioritize tasks, knowing how to communicate effectively, showing good predisposition toward new things, being open to new ideas, and a willingness to volunteer to work on various projects. Of course all these traits are useful in making a good impression on your boss, but lacking any one of these can disproportionately impact how your senior colleagues will perceive you in the organization. In terms of male-female differences, women tend to keep a low profile and to think they must focus on doing a good job and that their efforts will be recognized, whereas men tend to be more active when it comes to demonstrating their qualities and contributions. To effectively create a good impression you must increase the visibility of your work and contributions. In a world so full of data, attention goes wherever it is guided. Men also tend to be bolder when articulating their opinions and 'predictions,' whereas women prefer to take a thorough outlook, i.e., gather all the information and examine it before giving their opinion."

In previous chapters we discussed how certain passive female traits, coupled with the traditional aspects of our culture, could work against us in what's needed to achieve our goals. Knowing what you want, what you're worth, and what you bring to the negotiation table, are still key elements for obtaining the visibility Arturo mentioned above.

THE VOICE OF EXPERIENCE

"If you don't contribute value in your boss' eyes, if push comes to shove, you'll be out on a limb."

—*Lucía Ballas-Traynor, cofounder of MamasLatinas.com*

Making Your Boss an Ally

A good strategy for keeping a productive relationship with your bosses is to make them your mentors and allies. Although I'll be talking in depth about mentors in another chapter, I simply want to mention that the majority of women I interviewed for this book typically had mentors who have been bosses or their bosses' bosses. As Gloria Ysasi-Díaz, Vice President of the Supply Chain at Grainger, says, "When your boss takes an interest in your development, in growing you and sheltering you, they are more able to impact what you do or not do in your career."

YOUR VOICE FROM SOCIAL NETWORKS

"Having worked for both men and women, the saying 'there are many ways to build a mousetrap [. . .]' turns out to be true. There are different ways of tackling a challenge and succeeding. I honestly believe if there were more male-female coleadership groups, these would certainly be more successful. In our organization, I colead our diversity area with a woman and we're constantly covering each other's blind spots to achieve a more successful diversity strategy."

—*Will Robalino, Product Controller at UBS, via Facebook*

According to numerous studies and surveys conducted in different countries, the majority of women (and men) prefer to have bosses that are men. My own research for this book confirms that data. This comes as sad news given that 2010 was the first time that the amount of women in the U.S. workforce surpassed that of men. This reality isn't promising considering there's a greater percentage of women graduating from colleges and preparing for leadership positions than ever before.

> ## YOUR VOICE FROM SOCIAL NETWORKS
>
> "In response to the question on whether there's any difference on how to create a positive impression with your boss if you're male or female, yes, there is a difference. I seldom enjoyed working with a female boss because women always take everything too personally. It's hard to find female bosses who can handle their employees simply with logic instead of emotions. I've come across some excellent female bosses but they were older and had more experience. Disagreements with male bosses tend to dissipate faster (it's only 'business'). Women often hold grudges more than men. It's a shame that not all women have learned to check their emotions at the door."
>
> —*Beatriz Quezada, Senior General Ledger Accountant at McCann Erickson, via Facebook*

What do we owe this pervasive male boss preference to? Anecdotal evidence shows that women are more competitive with each other, two-faced, jealous, unsupportive of other women in junior positions, and tend to be excessively emotional and rash. The problem with these perceptions is that they affect you as much as they do your female boss because if you want to be a leader, someone has to give you a chance. And if the perception that women are poor bosses extends to you, it'll be hard to obtain the position you desire. Not only must you learn to make a good impression on your female boss, you must also be in a constant state of self-observation to avoid falling prey to similar stereotypes.

What often happens is that several minority groups fall into a survival mindset and fight each other for that limited power they have access to. This not only happens in the modern workplace but with more primitive tribes who fight each other to death while another group remains in power. A similar phenomenon apparently happens with women.

I've come across this type of behavior from women more than once and it reflects great insecurity and a belief that the pie has a fixed size. But with this negative approach, if we were to cut that pie into slices, each one of us would get less than before. The truth is, when you include other women on your team, supporting them and helping them grow in their respective careers, you're expanding the pie for all women; you're contributing toward creating a work environment where it's normal to see women in executive positions.

And, once again, it all depends on how you use language to explain your lack of support toward other women. If you decide that helping others grow divides the "pie" of available executive positions into smaller slices for each one, you'll trigger actions to confirm such a statement. If, on the other hand, you decide that the pie expands for all women when organizations are compelled to give them greater opportunities in general, you will align your actions to that statement. The results achieved will vary greatly in one case versus the other.

At the 2012 Multicultural Women's National Conference, organized by Working Mother Media, Jennifer Allyn from Price Waterhouse Coopers questioned the reasons for women buying into the narrative that women are mean to each other. "There are not enough women executives out there for that to be the reason why women are not climbing the corporate ladder. That's just an excuse people use to avoid working on the real problem." I wholeheartedly agree with her and her suggestion that the one thing women could do is to praise one another in public and keep any negative comments private.

THE VOICE OF EXPERIENCE

"These differences between minority groups (or between women) are ineffective and hurt everyone. I don't think people should focus on that. The biggest problem is that groups in control feel uncomfortable with people who look different (gender, race, ethnicity, etc.) instead of thinking that the difference opens horizons. The main problem is not women's lack of skill sets but rather how to motivate the controlling group to change the existing balance. It's not that women need to change; what must change is the work environment. And one of the solutions is not to promote one person alone. You have to bring in a group of people who don't look like the rest. For example, bring three women into a group of ten men. Or three Latinas into a group of ten Anglo women. At the end of the day, this is the strategy that I've seen most successful."

—*Gloria Ysasi-Díaz, Vice President of Grainger Supply Chain*

A Good Dose of Empathy Toward Your Boss Is Very Beneficial

A good first step toward developing a deeper level of empathy toward your boss is understanding her personal history. So, in addition to what you may find out on your own, it's important to find opportunities to talk to her outside the office setting, in a more relaxed place. Maybe during lunchtime or in a taxi on the way to some event. The more you know about her life, her difficulties as a child (the messages *she* received!), her family situation, and her personal and career goals, the easier it will be to understand her and, therefore, treat her. For instance, a friend of mine who holds a top position in a media company had a boss for whom nothing she did was ever enough. What's worse, she used to mistreat her in public. Her stomach used to churn every time her boss called her into the office, and she was constantly anxious, all of which impacted her productivity. Over time she was able to find out that her boss had been abused as a child and the only way she felt comfortable was having absolute control over her team. Similarly, my friend also realized that she tended to overreact to such abuse because it brought back memories of her own alcoholic father for whom nothing she did was ever enough.

This goes back to an earlier exercise where you were asked to review messages you received very early on in life that when triggered now, as an adult, bring you back to that old place. Take a few minutes to add to your list a few phrases that travel straight to the gut when you hear them today. This way you'll be able to track their origin and acknowledge that these unsettling feelings are not stirred up by what your boss said to you yesterday but by the memory her remarks triggered.

YOUR VOICE FROM SOCIAL NETWORKS

"I once had a boss who was the human resources director of a quasi-governmental organization. She got so stressed out with some employees that she used to call them to her office and yell at them. Everybody heard her screams and knew to keep away from her because she was in a foul mood after those meetings. As I cared about my job, I tried to learn how to get her out of that mood instead of ignoring her like everybody else did. She had an ego that needed to be constantly praised (I later found out that during her childhood she hadn't been praised enough). My compliment could be as

simple as how nice she smelled or what a beautiful suit she was wearing. But I really got it right when I praised her smarts. She had gone through great efforts to get her college degree as an adult, but it was awarded by a college for working adults and not one with selective admission as other prestigious universities. Identifying this emotional need proved to be so effective that she never yelled at me, which raised my coworkers' eyebrows as to why she liked me so much. I didn't enjoy 'manipulating' her this way but you must always find a way to avoid conflicts in the workplace when you're working with such emotional and volatile individuals."
—*Beatriz Quezada, Senior General Accountant at McCann Erickson, via Facebook*

Forget Biases

If you start a relationship with a new boss believing women are terrible supervisors, it is likely you'll confirm your belief. Let's see how this sequence happens in language: You meet someone and at the very moment you meet that person your mind is going, "Hmm . . . she dyed her hair red, that color doesn't look good on her; she has a great complexion, but she's obsessed with her looks; she must be a control freak. I'm sure my previous boss told her I'm very independent and that she'll want to keep me on a short leash. I'll show her what she's up against . . ." etc., etc., etc.

In other words, there's no chance you're going to like this person because you've already gone through your own inner filters (based on your experience, beliefs, and emotions). In doing so, you didn't even listen to what she was saying. This is why you don't remember the name of someone you just met . . . ten minutes later. While she was saying her name you were having an inner dialogue similar to the above. Besides the conscious monologue there are other subtle factors like smells, hormones, and energies also at

136

stake during these exchanges. In addition, the other person is also having an inner dialogue about you. Consequently, you will act in a certain way with this person and she will act according to how you acted and treated her. Therefore, employees who hate their bosses create, in turn, bosses who are not thrilled with them. In relationships, you need two to tango and when your boss perceives your hostility it's likely that he/she will react with a pinch of hostility toward you, too.

YOUR VOICE FROM SOCIAL NETWORKS

"It makes no difference whether my boss is male or female. The strategy applied is the same: to understand and support his/her personal and professional motivations. And also learn how he/she works in order to reflect those expectations in my results." —*John Pout via LinkedIn*

To achieve better results, the first thing you must do is to try to set aside your biases when starting any relationship, which is very hard to do. Try to be present each time you interact with your boss. Breathe deeply from your diaphragm, instead of through your nose, to force yourself to focus on the here and now and lower your anxiety level. This simple exercise will help you relax and be more receptive to what others have to say. The idea is not to build an answer in your mind while your boss is talking but to actively listen to him/her. The sense of being heard is among the few things that make others feel important. If not, look at your own experiences. Don't you feel appreciated when your significant other listens to you and then acts accordingly? Think of your own remarks when admiring others: "I like him/her because he/she listens to me" or "he/she's a great listener."

THE VOICE OF EXPERIENCE

"Almost all my bosses have been male and I was lucky to have had excellent relationships with them all, both men and women. What's interesting is that my most difficult relationships have been with women colleagues. My theory is that some women see others as a threat and refuse to admit that we would all be more successful if we supported each other."

—*Terri Austin, Vice President of Diversity and Inclusion at McGraw-Hill Companies*

"I learned valuable lessons from my direct managers, many of whom were women. My two most admired managers were working mothers who seemed to balance it all with grace and dignity. They were great performers. They developed their employees. They were no-nonsense women who treated people decently and kindly. They gave me the opportunity to grow and make mistakes. And their dedication and support inspired me to be a better professional, a better mother, and a better person."

—*Daisy Auger-Domínguez, Vice President Organizational and Workforce Diversity at Disney ABC Television Group*

Chapter 9

Networking, That Miracle Word

Nora Bulnes is known in South Florida as a businesswoman, philanthropist, and leading community member. She has received countless awards and recognition for her relentless social work, particularly within the Hispanic community. She is the founder of *Selecta*, a successful thirty-year-old English-language magazine targeted at upscale U.S. Hispanics. Nora has not only grown her business in an exclusive market, but also devoted great efforts and energy to support multiple charitable institutions such as St. Jude Children's Research Hospital, The American Cancer Society, and the American Heart Association. In addition, she was among the pioneers in the fight against AIDS when the disease was still considered taboo. In 2001 she created the Hope and Dreams Foundation, her own nonprofit organization dedicated to making a difference in the lives of those less fortunate.

Q: *How did you venture into starting a magazine without previous experience in the publishing world?*

A: Back then I owned a boutique in Coral Gables and simultaneously ran a modeling school. Thanks to my clientele and relations I had the chance to help several charitable institutions. I moved effortlessly in the Miami community. Unfortunately the building where my store was located caught fire and I was forced to close my business and reconsider my future. When the fire incident occurred, my good friend Rafael Casalins—the former editorial director of the *Nuevo Herald*'s Gallery section—began encouraging me to publish a social magazine. Though I had no experience in that world, I was very interested in creating a medium to unify the Hispanic and Anglo-Saxon markets, and that's how *Selecta* was born. I was convinced there was nothing like it in the local market and I saw it as the perfect opportunity to do something totally innovative.

Q: *What were some of the challenges you faced as a businesswoman?*

A: The beginning was very hard. We started working out of my garage with a small editorial group while I was in charge of selling advertising space. There were constant challenges, but I always enforced my strong personality when faced with difficulties. One of the greatest challenges was being able to penetrate the barriers of the publishing industry, printing companies, and especially distributors. The latter, back then, only bet on well-established publications discouraging family-owned businesses interested in publishing small monthly quantities. From the very beginning, when one door opened, four others closed. I even recall personally distributing those heavy magazine boxes because we didn't have a team to take care of that. I also had to bear with the contempt of skeptics who didn't see *Selecta* as upscale as other magazines. But thanks to all those connections I had developed over the years, and the support the magazine received, I was able to move ahead.

Q: *You are a leading figure in South Florida's high society and beyond. How has networking influenced your success as a businesswoman?*

A: This has been the key to my success. Everything I have achieved to date has been thanks to the relationships I've developed throughout the years. When I started knocking on doors selling ads for the magazine, the first people I visited were friends, and they referred me to their friends, and so on. Thanks to my friends I was able to introduce the magazine into the English-speaking world from the very beginning. This had never been seen before because it was a Hispanic magazine. That's how I got involved with the high society in Palm Beach. A prominent group of ladies gave me a hand in that transcendental moment. I made great friends there that I still keep, like Donald Trump who recently (as in previous years) advertised in my magazine commending us on our twenty-ninth anniversary.

Q: *More women are opening up their own companies and keeping them as family-owned businesses. How were you able to grow financially while keeping the company as a small family business?*

A: What's been most important to me was involving my two children. Each of them has contributed something valuable which enabled us to grow the business. Michael is responsible for the sales department and is the magazine's current president. He took the magazine to an international level. Avelina is in charge of general management, overseeing all finance issues and making sure day-to-day matters are in order. It has also been critical to build a good team. I have an editor and an art director who fully understand the editorial concept of *Selecta*.

Q: *On a scale from 1 to 5 (1 being the lowest) do you consider yourself:*
A: a. Risk taker: 5
    b. Competitive: 5
    c. Ambitious: 4   (This has to do with my wish to grow and be successful in life.)

I'm sure you've heard the term "networking" thousands of times when it comes to the best way to find a job. It's true; according to several estimates, roughly 80% of jobs are found through contacts. A good network is useful not only when you're looking for a job but also throughout the course of your career. It keeps you abreast on all sorts of opportunities, and it's also a good source for potential employees.

During this stage of questioning your occupation and looking for your own way out, networking is one of the activities you can rely on to strengthen your goals. It's also one of the topics I talk about most frequently at companies and organizations and no matter the audience's professional level someone will ask me to explain the term. So before going on to talk more in-depth about how to become a successful networker, let me make a few distinctions regarding its meaning.

In the context of your professional career, networking is the art of establishing, developing, and maintaining mutually beneficial short-, mid-, and long-term relationships. For many cultures (among them Hispanic) there's a certain feeling of discomfort toward this notion. This attitude may seem contradictory when you consider that in Latin America it's hard to do anything unless you have the right contact in the right place. In the U.S. it's deemed acceptable to attend a friend's dinner party and exchange business cards with someone you just met that evening. Those private occasions are ideal for establishing that necessary level of trust to do business with your recently acquired friend. In fact, this is how I came to know many influential people in my life: at a party, a group outing after a conference, an event, in a television station's green room, etc. People like to do business within their same circle of friends or with others that share similar values or interests. When people get to know you while practicing some activity they enjoy—playing golf or tennis—or through friends they appreciate, or at a place where only a select group has been invited, you automatically become included in that circle. That's why I suggest that you never go out without your business cards.

What Does Networking Mean?

When you've earned many distinctions in a specific area you may act and therefore also obtain productive results in that field. But if when someone says, "You've got to expand your network," you take it to mean going to every single event and exchanging business cards, you'll obtain one type of result. If, instead, your idea of networking includes a set of more explicit elements, you'll obtain results more akin to your expectations.

So, if you wish to develop a sound and effective network, consider:

> Personally connecting to another individual, i.e., becoming interested in who that person is, what he/she is looking for, what he/she does.

> Identifying how you can help that person achieve his/her own goals. Generosity is always rewarded and helps you build your brand faster.

> Keeping your network going through regular contact either by phone, email, social networks or personal appointments.

> Following up on your promises (or what has been promised to you) to keep communication flowing, and always keep your word.

It's good to remember that during these social exchanges, what you're mostly doing is exchanging promises, statements, assertions, and gestures, etc. Sometimes we lose sight of the fact that everything that surrounds us has been built with words; if we use them incorrectly, we may destroy that which we most appreciate in the blink of an eye.

Though we're far removed from the era of bartering, networking essentially comprises a big exchange of favors. You must remember that if someone does you a favor (introduces you to one of his/her contacts, recommends you for a promotion, offers to introduce you to a client who could sign an interesting agreement with your company), it implicitly entails that at some point in time you'll return that favor.

There are times when you need to explicitly say you're doing someone a favor so that the person understands that what you're doing implies some "cost" and that the favor should be repaid in time. By doing so you're 1) protecting yourself from someone who may act nonchalantly, not acknowledging that what you just did for him was an important favor he'll have to somehow payback; 2) assuring that when you want something of the person who's asking the favor they'll be there to help in the future. For example, a colleague once asked me to introduce him to my contacts so he could offer his services as a speaker. It definitely was a big favor because it implied opening up doors to companies and organizations that could hire him. Since he coordinated a program at a university I was eager to present at, I said to him, "I'd be delighted to talk to you about that. In exchange, I'd love you to introduce me to people at the university who could invite me to lecture."

Though this open exchange of favors may initially cause you discomfort, consider this: acting as if everything you give is free, and not asking for what you want or need in due time will only make you feel resentful. If you can make your attitude visible (instead of letting it continue to be invisible), chances are you'll adapt well to this market and consciously adjust your way of thinking in terms of what it means to ask for what you want.

Recently a publicist I know sent me an email asking if I knew someone at a large radio company. She wanted to know if the company was interested in interviewing a musician she was representing. By chance that same week I had met the right person for her to talk to. I immediately introduced them via email. Five minutes later, the publicist sent a message to my contact asking him if he wished to interview the musician. She then wrote me another email asking for my radio contact's phone number. Now, I had just met the radio company man and started a relationship in hopes of doing something together in the future. I decided to run the risk of introducing someone to him who just wanted "to sell him something" because I considered that my acquaintance could be offering something my contact might be interested in. To me that was a great favor. Yet, since the publicist didn't step into my shoes she was already asking me for a second favor (his phone number) which I denied. You must strike a balance between opening up your network to others and keeping the integrity of your personal brand. If I wanted this man to keep considering me a person he could do business with in the future, I couldn't run the risk of letting my acquaintance harass him with calls to insist on something he might not be interested in. I wanted to give him the chance to decide on his own whether he wished to interview the musician or not. In doing so I had to wait until he answered the email so that he could personally pass his phone number to the publicist. Which he did two days later.

Though I'm prone to taking on the broker role as the one making the introductions, the publicist example enables me to speak to you about a critical networking point: your reputation is intimately connected to the impeccability of your word. Whenever you recommend or introduce an important contact of yours to someone, you're putting your reputation on the line. Why? Because if I recommend Alice for that job opening as human resources director and you hire her and Alice quits two months later because she had a better offer, her behavior somehow impacts me because I recommended her. Afterwards, it's likely you won't be interested in the people I recommend to you in the future, impacting the rest of my network whose possibilities of connecting to you have been closed.

If I introduce you to a website designer and you retain his services and the man never delivers on time, or never answers your calls, I'm the one who loses face. This impacts me not just because I recommended someone who was a waste of your time and made you lose credibility with your own boss or clients due to the late delivery, but also because you might assume I approve of this kind of low-quality work ethic.

- -

THE VOICE OF EXPERIENCE

"Once, a Hispanic professional organization asked me to help them secure a CEO of a large corporation as keynote speaker at one of their conferences. The speaker was a friend of mine and he accepted. But the organization failed to make arrangements to pick him up at the airport or for hotel accommodations, so my friend called me up and told me not to ask him any more favors for that organization. I was very upset and promised myself not to help them out again. But a few years later they asked me to help them access another corporation. I was foolish enough to accept but under one condition: they shouldn't ask for sponsorship money because the company had just received bad news about a significant drop in their listed stock. The CEO had told me, "I accept to meet them but please tell them not to ask me for money." Well, could you believe that when we arrived at the meeting, the first thing they uttered to the CEO was that they needed money? From then on I never helped them again."

—*Miguel Alemañy, Director Global Baby Care, Procter & Gamble*

- -

It's important to be generous but you should also know what you can offer and to who. I used to be very open with my network years ago but, over time, as I include people of increasing hierarchy I've been forced to allow access only to those individuals that I know well and deserve my trust. And when I don't know the person asking for the favor well, but I consider it a good idea for that person to meet my contact, I first ask my contact for permission and only after they've approved do I go ahead with the presentation.

And, lastly, I'd like to point out that if in this world of favor bartering you become known for being the first to do a favor, you will naturally attract people who'd like to help you. On the contrary, if people discover that you only ask for favors and very seldom pay back, your reputation will soon be affected and it'll be much harder to achieve your goals. Unfortunately, younger generations don't consider this an important issue. They believe that because they're young they have a right to ask without taking on the responsibility they owe to those who have helped them out. Some don't realize that every time you're given something you must give something back in return. Others think they have nothing to offer. We all have something others want, whether it's ideas, time, resources, friends, contacts, knowledge, or some special skill we can teach. If you think along these lines, you'll notice how much faster your network expands.

THE VOICE OF EXPERIENCE

"I arrived to the U.S. in 1979 through a grant from the Inter American Press Association. In my suitcase I brought a letter of recommendation from the former President of Colombia, Alfonso López Michelsen. I had been confronting him for three years but when an unfair accusation was made against him, I had previously done my homework and knew that what they were saying wasn't true. I took the evidence and sent it to the newspaper *El Tiempo* and was able to prove the accusation was wrong.

As a result the President and I became friends. He came to the town where I was living and practicing as a newspaper correspondent to unveil his father's bust and when he came, he asked about me. That's how I got to know him in person. From then on, the regional governor took care of anything the town needed. If a school needed desks, he would send them. Or I would say 'such and such a road is full of potholes,' and he would send the bulldozers. One day, when the President found out I was coming to the U.S., he asked me to go to his home and take something to Miami. He gave me a closed letter for Arturo Villar. The letter said that I was one of the best writers he had ever known and recommended me for a job. He gave me a letter of recommendation but I didn't know. I brought the closed letter and delivered it to the person it was addressed to and that's how I found out its contents."

—Beatriz Parga, journalist for Candelero, a popular entertainment column published by several U.S. Hispanic newspapers and author of La Maestra y el Nobel, a book about Gabriel García Márquez's teacher

Assess Your Network to Know Where You Need to Expand Your Contacts

Before spending time and effort expanding your network, it's a good idea to assess who makes up your current network. This allows you to identify areas needing reinforcement.[1]

Fill out the form below with as many names as possible in each category. Think about who you know—and who knows you—within your department, division or within your company as a whole, as well as those outside the workplace. Include your peers, people in senior positions, and people in junior positions. If you own your own business, it's even more important to study who is within your network because as a businesswoman you should constantly be on the lookout for new clients. If you x-ray your network, you'll be able to identify where you need to expand and thus

1. This evaluation is adapted from the one created by my admired colleague Rosanna Durruthy, current Chief Diversity Officer of Cigna, for use with clients of her company Equus Group.

create a strategy according to your goals. Once you're finished, take a look at the questions following the table below.

	In your group/division	In your company	Outside your company
Junior			
Peer			
Senior			

When examining your contacts "map" do you notice:

> Some boxes are empty?
> A larger number of contacts in certain categories?
> Contacts with the same skill set? (For example, the majority are advertising people or engineers.)
> You have a lot of acquaintances in the same industry? (Most likely your own?)
> The majority of contacts know each other?
> The majority of people on your contact list share your ethnic/cultural background?
> Some of these people could be your mentors, sponsors, advocates or advisors?

When I do this exercise in my workshops for professional network development I always notice how it causes participants to look at their contact list in a new way. Not only do you notice where the gaps are, but you also realize how important it is to have a diverse network. If all your contacts know each other, this reduces the value you can contribute as a networker. If all your contacts have the same skill set you're limiting access to diverse talent—and to connections that diverse talent might have—which may help in solving future problems and even in keeping you abreast of opportunities in other departments or companies. If you only know people in your own department or company, the day you decide to leave or lose your job due to a reorganization, it'll be harder to find a job elsewhere. Besides, knowing people from other sectors opens up the possibility of adapting other companies or industries' ideas to yours.

Moreover, having contacts in high and low places is critical. More often than not the people who open doors and keep you updated on a company's unwritten rules and what happens in various departments at all levels are typically those lower down the ladder. Secretaries and administrative assistants are the gatekeepers. If you develop a good relationship with them, they may get you a meeting with their bosses that would otherwise take months of futile calls.

And I also want to touch upon one last point regarding your network composition. It is more than natural that each one of us moves within a social circle we feel comfortable in. This started off early on when you were a child and played with your schoolmates who lived close by, and it extends throughout your formative years up until adulthood. The end result is that we end up living in homogeneous circles with people who are like us. So that in the U.S., Hispanics tend to socialize with other Hispanics, Anglo-Saxons with Anglo-Saxons, blacks with blacks, etc. In Latin America this self-discrimination happens by social class. This creates an illusion that we live in a diverse society. In truth, diverse groups coexist in separate circles. If your dream is to access the highest power positions, you'll have no other option than to leave your comfort zone and socialize with white men and women who are the ones currently occupying upper level positions.

In doing so, it's important to identify which professional associations you should become a member of within your industry or interest area; what events and galas you should attend; the non-profit organizations and foundations you should support financially or volunteer for, etc. Sometimes it's easier to break the ice if you start with a friend or colleague. And although it's likely that at first you'll feel out of place or uncomfortable, the more you meet with this social group, the faster you'll find your place in it.

Making Distinctions in Your Network: Mentor, Sponsor, Advocate, and Advisor

Though the following chapter is devoted to this topic, I'd like to share a few distinctions with you now for expanding your network.

Mentor: A person who guides you in aspects related to your career/job development. A mentor may be formal or casual and at different hierarchical levels provided that he/she is an expert you respect in the area in which you seek guidance. (For instance, many companies match more experienced people with newly hired employees to guide them from the beginning on how the company operates. Others pair young juniors with executives to teach them how to use social media tools.) Depending on the areas that you are looking to develop, you may want to have more than one mentor. If you own your own business, you might look to other businesspeople as mentors, individuals who have sound companies and can share their experience on how to get government contracts, how to become certified as a Woman Owned Business or Minority Owned Business, and how to manage employees, etc.

Sponsor: If you hold a mid-level position or higher, a sponsor is a person who is at the top of the ladder in your company or in a key position in your industry who may not know you personally but follows your career or knows of you and your achievements.

They're the person who suggests your name whenever a good opportunity comes along, and who can open up doors that were closed earlier. If you are at a lower level, a sponsor can be a mid-level manager who can suggest opportunities for your career development.

Advocate: This individual may hold any job level and is someone who speaks well of you in your absence. Although sponsors are also your advocates, it's not quite the same. An advocate admires and respects you and acts like your cheerleader. They cooperate in building your reputation by commenting on your latest initiative, pointing out how well you treated someone, the opportunity you gave him/her, how much you help the community or how you're always willing to help others with their projects. I've acquired numerous clients thanks to advocates I met at conferences who recommended me to their bosses. They can be as important as sponsors!

Advisor: This person can be an acquaintance, friend or colleague who knows you well and who you can trust to inquire about specific topics you need help with. It may be timely to choose a board of advisors to seek advice on issues concerning your personal brand. Some of these advisors are hired professionals, like an agent or a lawyer; others provide advice out of good will or in exchange for a service you can provide. For example, I have a career advisor who helps me establish and meet my goals; a producer who advices me on media issues; a lawyer, a literary agent, an agent for my media career, etc.

- -

THE VOICE OF EXPERIENCE

"Academically and professionally, my two most memorable mentors were African American males. My grad school professor, Walter Stafford, dedicated his career to race and gender equity and instilled in me a deep sense of respect and appreciation for fighting the good fight and seeking equity and social justice in all I did. A graduate member of the Board of Coro New York Leadership Program, a leading civic organization, who saw something in me and thoughtfully tried to guide me professionally, gave me the most practical and sound advice on how to advance in corporate America, 'Position yourself as a revenue generator because that enhances your value. Don't go into HR.' I ended up borrowing lessons from both and building a career foundation on the business side which translated into a successful transition to CSR (Corporate Social Responsibility), diversity and inclusion. On a practical note, my mentors have also served as conduits of information, sponsors internally and externally, and have helped promote me in their internal circles."

—Daisy Auger-Domínguez, Vice President Organizational and
Workforce Diversity at Disney ABC Television Group

How to Socialize Professionally When You're an Introvert

At all my presentations on networking, there's always someone who sheepishly asks, "How do you network when you're an introvert?"

My **first** suggestion is to rethink the definition of "introvert" and consider that it's not written in stone that introverts cannot socialize and have a sound network. Start by creating a new story for yourself where you can rewrite the definition of introversion to adapt to your new goals. You may include things such as: an introvert is a person who respects his/her need to spend some time alone every day. They're individuals who value insight for creating their own opinion to later share with others when socializing. You may also include the idea that we all have a certain degree of introversion and yours is a little greater than most. This new story means that you can finally enjoy a certain degree of extroversion as well. In doing so, you're moving away from a trait that may have been determined for you by others early on and that you think you should continue identifying with.

When I asked Miguel Alemañy, Global Director of Baby Care, to comment on attendee participation at workshops conducted for the R&D department at Procter & Gamble—comprised of mostly engineers and scientists—he said, "According to the Myers Briggs test, 70% of this department's employees are introverts. Yet, everybody knows that in this company you won't be able to advance if you're an introvert. So everybody works to overcome that trait and step out of their comfort zone."

This is not only the case at Procter & Gamble but at all companies. These introverted employees struggle between remaining hidden at their desks hoping for someone to notice their efforts and reward them, or stepping out of their comfort zones and venturing into the world of networking where they can make their achievements known. In so doing, they can also help others grow while gaining greater visibility in their own careers.

The **second** suggestion is a specific strategy. Identify one or two people in your trusted circle of colleagues, who complement your style and respect what you do, and plan to attend more conferences and events with them. Obviously, the secret lies in not talking to your two friends in a corner the whole time, but to network and introduce yourselves to others. For example, with a television producer friend of mine I often do the following: she introduces me—she can speak highly of my achievements so I don't have to sound presumptuous doing so—and I introduce her. This works wonderfully for everybody (not only for shy individuals) because it gives the person you're introducing greater credibility. This goes to show why someone usually introduces speakers at conferences rather than having the speakers introduce themselves. The individual making the introduction may praise the speaker's awards, influence, and even fame-granting worthiness, which is harder to achieve on your own.

And while we're at it, let me divert you from your own introduction for a moment and make some recommendations for when it's your turn to introduce someone before a large audience at a conference or event. It's a unique opportunity to show your admiration for that person who will most likely be grateful to you and will take interest in adding you to their network. The complete opposite will happen if you don't know what to say about the person you're introducing. By all means you want to avoid just giving the speaker's name, adding one or two irrelevant facts, and concluding with something like, "I'll let you introduce yourself" or "I don't want to take time from your presentation by reading your bio." Make sure you take time to prepare what you're going to say beforehand.

I have an acquaintance I work well with when we introduce contacts to each other via email or phone. I've invited her to several events where I introduced her to countless relevant individuals for her career. Yet, every time I accompany her to some event she make no efforts to introduce me to her acquaintances. She alternates between ignoring me when I stand beside her and the person she's talking to, or she reluctantly introduces me minimizing my trajectory. This is not to say that your friend should exaggerate or lie, but look at the difference between these two introductions:

> ➤ I'd like you to meet Marisol González, sports producer for HBO Latino. She's working on her own documentary about children who are abandoned by their parents in the Mexican border. She's been invited as a special keynote speaker to several international film festivals.
> ➤ This is Marisol González. She's a sports producer for a cable station.

Do you see the huge difference between these two introductions? There isn't a trace of false advertising in either, but the first one paints a much more promising picture of Marisol whereas the second one doesn't say much to distinguish her from thousands of other people who work in television. This kind of carelessness is unpleasant for the person being introduced and might be a reason to strike you off their contact list, or get back at you for the slip in the future.

When you go to an event with one or two people you know it's easier to mingle and get to know more individuals. But what if you can't go with someone you know? In that case look for an opportunity to strike up a conversation with someone. Good places to consider: the line during registration, inside the conference room before the presentation begins, in line to purchase your meal, or in the restroom. Start with small talk like, "is this your first time at the event?" or "great to be out of the office for a few hours!" and try to establish a connection. After a while you may invite your new acquaintance to explore the event with you and meet other people. This makes you focus on getting to know one person at the event, the one you'll meet many others alongside. At the same time, it frees you from the stress of having to start up a dozen conversations, and it might even be more fun.

Another excellent strategy, especially if you're an introvert, is leveraging social media for making connections and keeping them. Once you've mastered this tool, and after you reinforce the relationship with some face-to-face meetings, you may minimize the need to appear at events you don't feel comfortable attending.

Using Social Networks to Expand Your Network
The rapid growth of social networks has opened a world of possible contacts. Nowadays I can find people who can help me with

any project anywhere on earth. To reach them I just have to search my LinkedIn account to see who knows who. But as fascinating as it sounds (and *is* when all works well), it is equally delicate a tool; because those names you see on the screen and that you call "friends" are really mostly strangers who now have access to your entire network, just as you have access to theirs. You must conscientiously decide who you'll accept as friends for your account—and the level of privacy you'll choose for your different networks— because you're enabling direct access to any of the contacts you went through great efforts to develop. If you don't know the individuals you're allowing to communicate freely with your network, you may regret it.

Moreover, if you yourself forget this part and act as if you're really close with your "online friends" and start asking favors of them, you might easily skip over a very important step for the relationship to run smoothly: **establishing mutual trust.**

Recently, through my initiative Latinosincollege.com, a website offering Latinos the resources they need to graduate from college, I've met countless of wonderful students and professionals that I currently work closely with. But with each person I went through a process similar to the one you go through when you first meet someone at a conference or meeting. Let me show you an example. When I launched my website in February 2009, Christine LeViseur Mendonça, a young woman finishing her MBA in Florida emailed me saying she wanted to be part of the initiative. She started off as one of our ambassadors helping to get the word out. Just like the majority of our ambassadors, I only communicated with her via email or by phone. She participated in several conference calls with other program ambassadors and shared a great deal of interesting ideas. Soon after, she traveled to New York looking for work and I invited her to participate in two presentations I was scheduled to do. I thought she might be able to meet several important people and made sure to introduce her to my contacts in the finance area. As the months went by our relationship grew stronger and Christine told me she wanted to take on a more active role in Latinos in College. After speaking with the rest of my team about how much Christine had contributed to the group, we all agreed she would be a valuable addition. Since then she serves as our operations director and has greatly contributed to our growth.

Due to our platform's large online component, I have hundreds of examples like Christine's where initial contact is made via the Internet. In this case it was extremely important to develop mutual trust with someone I had met online first before doing business with them. As I mentioned earlier, difficulties arise when you skip a step and ask someone who doesn't even know who you are (because that someone accepted your request to be friends via LinkedIn without thinking twice,) to introduce you to someone in their company. Or even worse, when you ask that person who doesn't really know you if they have work opportunities for you. The same happens when you join a Facebook group and, before familiarizing yourself with its dynamics, ask for something you need. Nobody likes to feel their trust has been violated. Rules governing online relationship building are the same as those in the real world: you have to first earn the trust and respect of friends and acquaintances before creating an effective professional network.

Another productive way of finding online contacts is by joining professional or industry association interest groups and discussion forums. By frequently contributing with comments, the community gets to know you; sharing relevant information and answering questions sets you apart as a leader within that space. And remember you must always try to strike a balance between seeking to connect with individuals you're interested in and achieving necessary visibility for others to find you. You can do this by producing content: writing blogs, creating videos or finding other creative ways of having a web presence.

How to Ask Your Social Media Contacts to Introduce You to Their Contacts

A popular online mechanism for expanding one's network is browsing your friend's contact list and requesting an introduction. For example, if you're friends with John Lenz via LinkedIn and you see that Lisa Smith from Acme is in his network and you'd like to meet her, you could ask John to introduce her to you. But this type of request must be handled very carefully so as not to hurt your relationship with John for trying to reach Lisa. What must you consider? Mainly, how well you know John to ask him for a favor. If you don't know him well enough, I recommend not asking him, and even less so if Lisa has a prominent position at Acme. The majority of people will not risk their own reputation with someone from their network (John with Lisa) for a third party they hardly know. Just like in a real-life relationship, using your common sense and stepping into the other person's shoes (i.e., how would you feel if someone asked you to introduce them to someone like Lisa from your network) is the best way to avoid developing a bad reputation. You must consider that when you ask for an introduction, the person who accepts doing it is dedicating some time to it, placing their reputation on the line for you, and is "using" a contact they might rather "keep" for a better purpose. How well does John know you to spend the time, put his reputation on the line, and "use" his contact for you?

How and When to Keep in Touch

Successful people know that keeping in touch periodically with one's network is key to maintaining those relations. Luckily, in this day and age, with so many communication options, it's become much simpler. Sending an email every so often to ask how your contacts are faring, or sharing a video or relevant article (and watch out not to do it too often since we all live overwhelmed by inboxes) are effective ways of reaching out. You could also opt for calling, texting, or sending them a quick message via Facebook, LinkedIn, or Twitter. And never forget that meeting in person assures quality time. With some people, meeting once a year at some event you both attend is enough to reinforce the relationship. With others, you'll attain better results meeting for lunch once every three to four months.

The frequency and type of contact you choose to have depends on the relationship. For instance, if you have a distant relationship with someone who is high up the ladder, it's not a good idea to text them or post a message on their Facebook wall where they communicate with close friends and family. Generally speaking—and this piece of advice is particularly directed to younger readers who aren't used to more formal communication—with older and/or high-ranking individuals it's best to contact them via email, phone or a handwritten card.

Different Ways of Networking: Men and Women

You may have noticed that men typically have broad social networks filled with people they have a relatively superficial relationship with. It could be other men they grab a beer with after work to talk sports and all sorts of business, or a group they play ball with once a week. What's interesting is that for them asking favors of individuals they've just met or acquaintances of those individuals, isn't as complicated. Without hesitating they ask their new connections if they're interested in arranging a sales meeting so they can show them the product they're promoting. Their strength resides in having a large network and the freedom to resort to it at any time.

Conversely, women tend to develop deeper relationships and don't feel as free asking favors of people they've just met. The advantage in this is that women are more likely to surround themselves with people who are willing to take risks on their behalf. Yet, it's important to incorporate both kinds of connections into your networking approach because you never know who will support you when you're in need. Often, though you might not always be aware of it, people you meet at an event who aren't necessarily your friends end up being the ones who remember you when a job opportunity arises or the ones to recommend you to their executive friends.

For instance, to try to get in contact with some of the celebrities I interviewed for this book, I reached out to both my closest friends and more distant colleagues. Ultimately, a close friend introduced me to an acquaintance of hers who opened up all doors even before we became great friends. The secret to getting your network to respond is to be known as a person who helps others whenever they need you. Thus it's understood—according to networking's unwritten rules—that when you need something they'll be there to help you get it.

- -

THE VOICE OF EXPERIENCE

"I help people because I like to. But there are people who I helped a lot and when, at a given time, I called them to ask for help, they said they were unable to help out. I deleted them from my network."

—*Miguel Alemañy, Global Director of Baby Care, Procter & Gamble*
- -

The Art of Storytelling

Have you ever noticed that those with the most diverse networks tend to be flat out interesting people? Look who has the largest number of followers on Twitter or readers following their blogs (or have a circle of listeners around them at a party) and you'll see that these individuals not only know how to choose their topics, but also know how to capture an audience by telling captivating stories. You'll find storytelling is not only useful for expanding your network but for seeking project support or in negotiation. The manner in which you present your case about why your bosses should give you that raise or that budget will greatly determine whether you get it or not. To obtain positive results, it's crucial to understand the basic elements of a good story and apply them with a touch of your own personal style.

♥   ♥   ♥   ♥   ♥

Practical Storytelling Guide

As a short story writer, this tool has been very useful throughout my life and career. But you don't have to be a writer to find your own voice as a storyteller. Latinos tend to provide ample context when talking. Though this may prove inconvenient in a professional setting, socially it's an advantage. With a little practice, you'll be telling stories like the pros in no time. For a story to be effective you must:

- Choose topics appropriate for your audience and circumstances. To avoid an inappropriate subject or tone, be conscious of the context you're in.
- Identify interesting stories as you experience them and write them down. Then practice telling a summarized version for your friends.

- A good story must have interesting characters; a plot (even if brief) must have a beginning, middle, and end. The tension (i.e., something that creates expectation) should be resolved at the end, and if the ending is unexpected or funny, all the better. And don't forget to cover the *who, what, where, when, and why* in your story.
- If using humor, I suggest not directing it to any minority group in particular, unless you yourself belong to one. And, typically, humor is well accepted when it's self-deprecating.
- Estimate the time it takes you to "get to the point" to avoid losing the audience's attention.
- Connect the stories you tell to the subject matter of the event you're attending. For instance, during my presentations I tell countless anecdotes related to the topic at hand making it more interesting and practical.
- At a social setting (and without being gossipy), the secret in capturing the attention of a larger group lies in being able to tell stories where others are the protagonists instead of you.

With a little practice storytelling will become second nature and you'll become an invaluable member of your network.

♠ ♠ ♠ ♠ ♠

To close this chapter I'd like to quote an article published in *Administrative Science Quarterly*. A 2000 study researching the effects of personal traits in economic compensation found that in terms of salary, people who had a close connection with at least one person within the organization were able to negotiate wages 4.7% higher than those who had no social bonds. I hope this statistic will solidify your decision to begin broadening your professional circle today.

Chapter 10

Mentors, Sponsors, Advocates, Advisors, and Private Coaches

Famous Women Speak: Carolina Bayón

Carolina Bayón is Director of International Cooperation and Policy of the U.S. Olympic Committee (USOC). She has been involved in the Olympic Movement for fifteen years and has traveled to over sixty countries on the five continents. Carolina earned her degree in journalism, majoring in public relations and business administration. Born in Colombia and raised in the U.S., she started her career with internships at the White House press office, HBO, and Univision.

Q: *What was your trajectory before joining USOC?*

A: I started out as an intern in the U.S. Olympic Committee right after working as an intern in the White House during President Bill Clinton's administration. In college I had also done some internship work at Univision's news program in Miami and at HBO in New York. The intern group at USOC was large but at that time there was no one who spoke Spanish, and I was pretty fluent. Spanish was always spoken at home because my mom believed in the importance of having bilingual children. As a result, during my internship at the USOC I was lucky to be chosen to support our team in Argentina during the Pan American

Games. So, I've had a long trajectory with the Olympic movement, including my work within the Olympic Games' organizing committees in Sydney and Salt Lake City. I also worked with the International Olympic Committee in Lausanne, Switzerland, for almost five years before accepting my current position at the international relations department of the U.S. Olympic Committee.

Q: *I know you have moved a few times for work opportunities. How much has your willingness to move and travel helped your career?*

A: I always thought that being in contact with other cultures nourishes you in many ways. Having worked in Australia and Switzerland has given me an array of possibilities because I had a better understanding of the needs and the people who run this great world sports movement.

Q: *The sports world is often viewed as male-dominated. Was it hard to earn your place?*

A: Fortunately, people respect my work. So this hasn't been a drawback. Perhaps it's because I see people on an equal footing and don't discriminate against one's gender, beliefs or culture. I myself have been perceived that way by people who share the same ideals. Being a woman hasn't been an issue for me, and I've been able to attain personal fulfillment thanks to my husband's support in taking care of the kids.

Q: *Have you had sponsors in your professional life, i.e., top executives who acted as sponsors and opened up doors? And how about mentors?*

A: There's something very important in life and that is, even when you think you're performing a task that nobody notices, there's always someone who does notice when you're doing a good job. Being concerned about performing that task well has been instrumental for me.

Likewise, if I see someone doing a good job and who is interested in the Olympic Movement, I recommend them for specific positions; even to replace me when I've had to move to another country. At some point in time, Peter Ueberroth, Chairman of the U.S. Olympic Committee, told my new boss that he had made an excellent choice in hiring me. This type of support behind closed doors has added more importance and trust to my work within the organization. My mentors have been my bosses in different organizations. I've always learned a great deal from them. This job demands 100% of you and, fortunately, all the people who participate in the Olympic Movement are aware of this requirement.

Whatever the path you've decided to tread, it's likely that there'll be areas where you need to develop new distinctions to achieve your goals. The best way to gain support for your journey is having a group of individuals serving specific roles within your network.

Quite often, when I ask a group to assess their networks and we come to the question of identifying people who are or could be their mentors, sponsors, advocates or advisors, these terms wind up sounding new to many. You yourself—up until the previous chapter where I explained them—may have not been aware of their distinctions as well. Which means that it's likely you haven't deliberately found individuals to fill those roles in your career. If these distinctions weren't clear to you, then you couldn't "see" these roles, and, therefore, were unable to act on them. Now that you do, you can go ahead and begin the search.

1. What Is a Mentor?

Within this context, a mentor is a person who guides you in aspects relating to your career development. It may very well stem from the role old masters played while teaching different trades to their apprentices. Each craftsperson or member of a trade received direct instructions from his/her master. Even to this day, this type of relationship still takes place in Latin America and in other areas of the world. At other levels, however, mentors in Latin America are often part of a greater mechanism to keep social classes apart. In other words, children of privileged classes have mentors who ensure their continued access to educational and professional circles, whereas individuals from lower socio economic classes don't have access to such mentors. If your parents grew up in Latin America, they probably passed down a similar belief during your upbringing.

Conversely, in the U.S. mentors contribute to lessening the gap between individuals from differing social classes and cultures. In recent years, the U.S. has seen an increase in the amount of formal mentorship programs being offered within corporations. Today, with the help of technology, mentors and protégés can be matched by their list of traits. Some will have mentors in remote locations, while others work in the same building.

During the course of your career you may choose to have one or more than one mentor simultaneously. Your relationship can be formal or informal (i.e., you and your mentor agree that they will be taking on that role and that you'll be meeting from time to time to be mentored); your mentor can be anywhere on the corporate ladder provided that they're an expert you respect in the field and that you're receiving guidance; and they can be of any race, gender, or sexual orientation. In other words, a mentor doesn't need to share any of your characteristics.

THE VOICE OF EXPERIENCE

"By and large my mentors, both formal and informal, were male. I think that is a function of the time that I worked in administrative positions. That may not be the case today, but it certainly was in my experience in the late 1980s. My mentors weren't of my race/ethnicity [African American] either."

—Carol Franks-Randall, retired public school superintendent,
Elmsford, New York

How to Find a Mentor

If you work for a large company, it's quite common for your boss to be your mentor. To illustrate this point, Cristina Vilella, Marketing Director at McDonald's USA and retired Lieutenant Colonel of the U.S. Air Force says: "In the Air Force I had mentors who were neither women nor Latino. My immediate boss became my formal mentor. I was looking for feedback on how to improve the organization and what change I could bring about. Later on at McDonald's I looked for other women in similar positions who were Latina or from other minority groups to help me navigate the organization. Thank God the Air Force had a formal mentor program and that's how I got started. As an officer, I also found myself mentoring many enlisted women and Hispanics. So I was identifying talent and being a mentor while someone else was mentoring me. This was very helpful because when you understand what others need from their mentor, you understand what you need yourself, stuff you don't realize on your own. Being a mentor entails great responsibility."

The majority of my interviewees claimed mentors who were also their bosses (and their boss's bosses). And the good thing about bosses is that they know exactly how your company operates. Yet, you mustn't dismiss the validity in finding other mentors from outside divisions or different companies. They can also offer you different viewpoints or suggest other roads for achieving your goals. Since there's no limit to the number of mentors you can have, I suggest you explore beyond your bosses. To accomplish that goal there's nothing like staying alert.

When my first book *How to Find a Job in the U.S.* came out, Julie Stav, a well-known personality in the finance field, invited me to speak on her radio show. The program we did was so successful that she continued receiving calls after we were off the air. In light of this she called me and offered advice on how to direct my career in the media. She was so generous that she even introduced me to her lawyer and asked him to be my mentor in the entertainment world. Julie became my informal mentor during the beginnings of my career and we continue to stay in touch by phone and meetings on an as-needed basis. In time, Julie wrote the prologue to my book *The Latino Advantage in the Workplace*.

If you work in a small company, look into becoming a member of an association within your industry where you can meet people you connect with, admire, and can learn from. I underscore the *connection* factor because without chemistry it's unlikely you'll develop a productive relationship with your mentor. If your mentor is willing to devote time and knowledge, they will only do so if there's an interest in you. This is why it's not effective to approach a total stranger and ask whether he/she would like to be your mentor. It's more advisable to first develop mutual trust (returning again to this valuable lesson) and formalize the relationship later on.

If you're a business owner, find other colleagues who own sound businesses to guide you in new areas you're interested in exploring. For example, if you're considering exporting your product or selling your services via the Internet, what could be better than establishing a relationship with someone who has already sold their product online successfully so you can avoid beginners' mistakes? You can also find potential mentors at industry meetings, your local chamber of commerce or on the online professional network LinkedIn.

THE VOICE OF EXPERIENCE

"When I was looking for a job, I met a woman through The National Arts Club, an organization where I was the head of the education committee. I was a professor at the time and was looking to switch careers when a friend introduced me to this woman. She was older and worked for Blue Cross Blue Shield. She interviewed and recommended me to a colleague who hired me. I started making twice as much money as I was making when I was a professor. She became my mentor and told me I would always work for her. The day I started work she was named President of Blue Cross Blue Shield. Later she became the Dean of the School of Public Health at New York Medical College and asked me to join her as an adjunct faculty member. I edited the school's journal and organized conferences for her even when I had a full-time job. I only stopped working for her when she passed away. It was a lifelong relationship that was incredibly fulfilling both inside and outside the professional sphere."

—*Esther R. Dyer, Ph.D., President and CEO of*
National Medical Fellowships, Inc.

How to Handle the Relationship

As in most relationships, each party has something to gain. A mentor derives great satisfaction from helping another person and seeing that person grow both professionally and personally. There are few things as rewarding as seeing one of your protégés succeed in their career and reach their potential. Moreover, mentors are exposed to valuable knowledge. Think of how a younger person can offer their mentor updated information on multimedia management, as well as new ideas and a fresh viewpoint. In addition, the relationship generates loyal allies.

But a productive relationship with a mentor requires certain formalities that fall on the protégé. These formalities relate to establishing your goals, complying with the tasks your mentor asks of you, managing the meeting calendar, and the agenda. All of which makes complete sense when you consider it's you who's in charge of your own career.

One day, I was approached by a young student I met through my Latinos in College initiative who I'd been supporting for a long time. He asked me to be his formal mentor. For our first meeting I asked him to list the goals with which he needed help. After telling me about them I asked him to fulfill several assignments and then send them to me. He asked when we'd meet again and I answered that first he had to finish the assignments I had given him.

I didn't hear back from him for several weeks. When he finally contacted me again it was to request another meeting. Since my schedule is pretty tight and he hadn't done what I had asked him to do, I suggested we talk by phone. Once more I highlighted the steps he had to follow and, again, he disappeared. Sometime later he reappeared with other issues he needed me to help him with.

This is not the optimal way to work with a mentor. We all have time restraints and prefer to use it wisely with someone who is serious about their careers. I'm sure you've experienced the frustration of wanting to help someone who doesn't want to be helped. So when you're the person asking for help you have to be ready to receive it.

If you formalize a relationship with a mentor—or even when you don't—and that person makes suggestions you don't follow, yet you continue asking for advice, the incentive to help you quickly erodes. This is not to say that you should follow all of your mentor's recommendations, but if you don't agree with some, you should discuss them and explain your point of view. But if you choose someone you trust, admire and respect within the area in which you need help, I don't think it's productive to disregard that person's advice, particularly when that person is trying to help you figure out your priorities. If you believe your mentor's advice is consistently inaccurate, it may be best to look for another mentor. If you feel reluctant because you're not used to acting in a certain way, examine your reactions and reflect upon them within the framework of language and predeterminations—those cultural mandates and messages—and see what you may unravel. Maybe your reluctance is related to something in your past which is no longer valid. For example, you might discover that it's hard for you to accept feedback because it reminds you of your mother's critical remarks.

THE VOICE OF EXPERIENCE

"I look for people I admire in terms of their professional life, philanthropic nature or their faith. My goal is to build a relationship with them. I pose a lot of questions and I listen. Then I listen some more. I listen not only to what they have to say, but what others say about them or about the topics under discussion. I take each person I meet as a learning opportunity. At that time I may not know how we'll be connecting, but I walk away having learned something new about that person or, very often, about myself."
—*Christine LeViseur Mendonça, Directing Manager of Shore to Shore Advisory, LLC and Operations Director of Latinos in College*

As a woman it's important to make sure your mentor (especially if male) doesn't become a paternal or an authoritarian figure you have a hard time disagreeing with. If you bear this in mind, you'll be less likely to fall into that trap. Given our experience both with our parents and the machismo in Latin America and other regions, it's almost natural that we take on a submissive position with our bosses and mentors. But the best way to way to grow in your career, and as a person, is through open dialogue that enables the exchange of ideas.

Arturo Poiré's Corner
✦

"There's a difference in how males and females relate to mentors of the opposite sex. For men, a mentor is like a sports coach who makes suggestions and directs them. Women tend to doubt themselves more and are less adept at taking on risks. And if they are Latina, they have the added element of being loyal, along with a particular relationship with authority, which results in a complicated concoction. Therefore, you must watch out at all times that the relationship isn't turning paternalistic so that you feel uncomfortable saying no to what your mentor suggests. For women who are less aggressive when it comes to fighting for their careers, having a strong mentor can make things difficult. There comes a time where you must reach decision-making independence. Besides, it's very important to have a roadmap of your career, to put your goals in writing, to go back to them regularly and verify whether you're taking appropriate steps to meet the goals you've set for yourself. Sometimes your mentor may suggest things that don't really match what you want for yourself. For instance, Ana, a very successful female executive who I coached, decided to leave her position in a large corporation because her boss saw a different road for her; though it was full of good opportunities, it was not the one Ana was interested in for her future. To arrive at that place you need to learn how to find your own voice, one you can trust. Unless you have a clear picture of what you want, your career will be guided by others. And here's the problem with corporate careers: everybody is always defining what they want for you. So, only if you have a plan which you must review every six months—like your investment portfolio—will you know if you're on the right track or whether you've detoured."

2. What Is a Sponsor?

Many times the concept of a mentor is confused with that of a sponsor, which is pretty understandable being that mentors frequently become sponsors. (And let me make it clear that in this context, the term sponsor has nothing to do with the person who contributes money to support a cause or promote a product.) Yet there are clear differences between the two roles and knowing them will allow you to search for the right individuals. Depending on your career level, a sponsor is a person in a higher position within your company or industry with whom you might not even have a close personal relationship. (If you are quite advanced in your career, then a sponsor for you would be someone in the highest echelons of your organization.) Yet, that person knows you, follows your career, knows about your achievements and believes in your potential. They're the person who suggests your name whenever a good opportunity comes along, and the person who can open doors that would otherwise be inaccessible. Sponsors help you build credibility and can help you save face if at some point you screw up. One of the great advantages of having sponsors is that they give you access to a network that is much higher up the ladder than yours.

The majority of top executives owe a substantial part of their success to the support of one or more sponsors throughout their careers. As I mentioned earlier, your mentor may sometimes act as your sponsor, as in Esther R. Dyer's case: the woman who hired her to work at Blue Cross served both as a mentor (guiding her during her transition from the academic world to the corporate sector) and as her sponsor as she continued to open doors for Esther in subsequent job positions.

THE VOICE OF EXPERIENCE

"But beyond mentoring, not enough attention is placed on the power of having a sponsor, someone who uses chips on his or her protégé's behalf and advocates for his or her next promotion, new job, etc., as well as doing at least two of the following: expanding the perception of what the protégé can do; making connections to senior leaders; promoting his or her visibility; opening up career opportunities; offering advice on appearance and executive presence; making connections outside the company; and giving advice. A lot has been done to offer useful advice to talented women. I strongly believe we are at a critical juncture where what is needed are corporate sponsors to help pull top talent up to the next level."

—*Daisy Auger-Domínguez, Vice President Organizational and Workforce Diversity at Disney ABC Television Group*

The bottom line is that sponsors are equally as important as mentors. In fact, a recent Catalyst study[1] showed that, compared to their male counterparts, high potential women are often *overmentored* and *undersponsored*. With too many mentors and few sponsors, these talents fail to undergo adequate career advancement.

How to Find a Sponsor

If you work in a large corporation, the process of finding a sponsor begins by making yourself known to the person holding the highest rank you can access. As Ruth Gaviria points out in the box be-

---

1. "Sponsoring Women to Success," Heather Foust-Cummings, Sarah Dinolfo, Jennifer Kohler. *Catalyst*, August 2011.

low, if you are high enough in your organization, your goal must be to get to know your chief executive officer, because CEOs of different companies (even more so in the same industry) know each other and exchange references with one another. Believe it or not, if you are at a high level in your career, the best way to find a job at another company in the future is by developing a relationship with the CEO at your current job.

THE VOICE OF EXPERIENCE

"I never got a job through an executive recruiter. I always got jobs through my network, and my most recent jobs came through my sponsor, who has recommended me for opportunities she found out about even before I did. When you work in a company it is imperative to know your CEO. What many people don't know is that once you achieve a director position or higher, you have the right to request a meeting with your CEO. The best way to go about it is to first talk to your boss and ask them if they think it's all right to do so. And I would go about it as follows, 'I heard our CEO talk at such and such event and I was so impressed with his vision that I'd like to meet him. Do you agree?' I would never deny an employee such an opportunity, on the contrary, it would make me think that person is interested in career advancement. Now, once you've secured that meeting, you must be prepared not just for those questions you'll be asking but for what the CEO might ask you. No CEO will miss the chance of listening to someone at a lower position in the company because, typically, immediate subordinates don't report to the CEO what goes on in the employee ranks. The first thing I always do is present my goals and explain what I do, and then ask something along these lines: What is your vision for my division? How can I help you meet those goals? What can I do to improve this position? And then, get ready for questions he will pose, like: What's your perception of the company morale? Where do you think new revenue will come from? How can we make our clients happier with our product/service/scheduling, etc.? The idea is not just to have answers on the tip of your tongue but to also offer solutions. And the best way of presenting solutions is humbly: 'I think what might work could be [. . .]' or 'I have a feeling we could try doing [. . .].' What you must realize is that very few people dare tell the CEO what is really happening at nonhierarchical levels in the company. You could be one of those people who'll keep him abreast of the news. You'd be someone who takes the pulse of the company and reports it back to him. This will give you a competitive advantage even if you aren't the only person doing it. And of course you must be very careful with the topics you discuss and who you talk about. You must never speak poorly of your boss or your boss's boss; that will only get you into trouble. My strategy has always been to ensure the CEO knows who I am and to ask him in the first meeting if I could report my progress once a year. As a result, I was able to use my former CEOs as references for each new job, which opened doors and got me hired over and over again."

—*Ruth Gaviria, Senior Vice President Corporate Marketing for Univision*

In fact, you could use the same strategy Ruth talks about to gain visibility with any other high ranking individual in your company or industry. If you work for a really large company, it's probably impossible to meet the CEO unless you are at an executive level. If this is the case, then meet with the chief diversity officer or chief marketing officer or the executive vice president of your division. What's important is to be prepared for that meeting, and, as Ruth suggests, not just to present what you do, but also to offer solutions to problems you've identified. It's also important to note that when you're in charge of employees, your conversation shouldn't necessarily be about you, but about your team. In order to be seen as a leader it is critical for you to speak like one, and leaders never talk about themselves but about what their team achieved under their leadership. (For more points of view on this topic, read the box where I share what five CEOs said to me about Ruth's suggestions.)

The same principle applies whether you own your own business or work at a small or midsized company. As a business owner, when you do an excellent job, your clients act as sponsors. For one, they promote you internally so that their companies offer you better contracts. They also recommend you to other firms who may use your products or services. If you work for a small company, establishing good relationships with the owners or general directors also increases your chances of being offered more opportunities. Make sure to also become a member of your industry's associations in order to meet executives from similar companies. You never know who will stick up for you.

How to Handle the Relationship

The principles used to build and maintain a professional alliance are similar to any kind of relationship: make sure to value the other person, show interest in what they do, in their goals, and follow up with them at regular intervals. When it comes to sponsors, although you won't be talking to them as often as you will with your mentors (and there will be some sponsors you might never talk to at all), that doesn't mean you can't establish contact points every six months or once a year as Ruth Gaviria suggests.

The higher your sponsor's level, the less likely you'll be able to connect to them as often. Yet, it's up to you to arrange regular meetings or talks where you can bring your sponsor up to speed regarding your situation. And when you finally have their attention, use the opportunity as a chance to offer your point of view on issues he/she brings up. Be sure to avoid becoming excessively demanding of your sponsor or expect answers from them that you should solve with your mentors. It would be a shame not to leverage this valuable relationship simply because you don't know how to handle it.

CEOs Talk

✦

I had the chance to talk to four CEOs and one COO (Chief Operating Officer) at a conference organized by Diversity Best Practices (www.diversitybestpractices.com).

I asked them what they thought about Ruth Gaviria's recommendations, namely that any employee holding a position as director or above should request an annual meeting with the company's top executive.

They all agreed that it was an excellent idea and most have established some kind of system to facilitate the connection between high-potential individuals and executives who could serve as mentors.

Michael Howard, COO of Army and Air Force Exchange Service, says that his agency, which handles service and product supplies, has an open door policy and that the appropriate protocol is for the person to tell his or her boss about wanting an interview with the COO or CEO. "I engage in a teleconference once a week with different groups in our company and I attend their events. That is, I try to keep in touch with non-hierarchical staff and listen to their needs."

John Edwardson, Chairman and CEO at CDW, an IT and service provider with a staff of six thousand employees says, "I have lunch on a quarterly basis with several groups of employees who are directors and above. We try to meet in groups because it's more efficient that way. During that meeting I learn about their progress and needs. But if someone requests an individual meeting, I schedule it for half an hour. One thing is for sure, if they come to talk to me, I don't want to hear them say 'I this' or 'I that.' At this stage, I want to hear them talk about 'us' and 'our achievements.'"

MARIELA DABBAH

Michael I. Roth, Chairman & CEO at Interpublic, one of the largest advertising and marketing companies worldwide says, "I have an open door policy. Anybody who wants to talk to me only needs to make an appointment." Several of his employees who were by his side while we chatted laughed and one added: "Or come to our events because he's always there."

John B. Veihmeyer, Chairman and CEO for KPMG, LLP, one of the five largest accounting firms in the U.S., says his company has Leaders Engaging Leaders, a leadership program, where each member of the board and each top executive takes a high-potential employee under their wing and mentors them. "In the majority of organizations, if you happen to be a diverse talent (Latino, African American, Asian, etc.) and request a meeting with a senior executive, I don't think anyone will say they're too busy. And although in my case letting your boss know beforehand that you have a meeting with me is not top priority, I suggest you do so. Because the first thing I do when someone asks to see me is contact that person's boss and ask about his or her performance, what that person is involved in, etc. It's not a question of asking your boss's permission, but rather simply saying, 'I just wanted to let you know that I sent an email to John and we'll be meeting on such a day.'"

George Borst, President and CEO of Toyota Financial Services, says he also meets regularly with his employee groups' leaders (Employee Resource Group or ERG). "One of those groups is the women's group, and right after our meetings there's always one or two women who send me an email thanking me for the meeting and asking me if I'd accept being their mentor. These may be women who are four levels below the CEO, and I always say yes to them. We meet for half an hour and I suggest what they should do. We then get together

180

three months later to check their progress. In a perfect world, they tell their bosses they're meeting with me. But the truth is that many of these women work for bosses who don't want them to meet with me. So then I become their accomplice and guide them as to what's the best way to work with their bosses. Maybe I'll tell their bosses about it after we've met. I believe women are too nice and humble and don't self-promote themselves. They don't give themselves enough credit. Typically, when men talk to me it's more likely that they'll mention twenty-five things they've done while women, even if they have done wonderful things, tend to share the credit for those achievements."

During a subsequent conversation with George we discussed topics that women who approach his office should consult him on. "Ideally, women should talk to me about issues related to the company's vision and strategy. They should be able to understand where I want to direct the company or the department where they work. I'd like them to show me how what they're involved in could help materialize my vision. Having said this, I have a lot of respect for people who challenge me. If I say, 'our aspiration as a company is to reach such and such a goal,' I'd like them to challenge me and explain their point of view; I'd like to have a conversation and once we reach an agreement, to see them working on how they will contribute to meet that goal."

Before closing this discussion, I'd like to add that it's crucial to understand your CEO and company's style in order to know the best way to approach him or her. And although some companies are more formal than others, it doesn't hurt to let your boss know that you'll be requesting a meeting with your CEO. If your boss disagrees with your meeting plan, several of the executives interviewed suggested you should communicate with them directly. By denying you the opportunity to meet with the CEO, your boss could be interfering with your advancement and this is a bad symptom for your company. Yet, in the real world, this move may generate a clash with your boss; so be sure to use diplomacy and caution in order to avoid creating enemies on your road to achieving greater visibility.

For many of the women I interviewed, having a sponsor made the difference between being stuck in their organizations and having moved ahead as they did. Gloria Puentes, National Director of the Dignity and Respect Campaign at the University of Pittsburgh Medical Center says that one way to increase female representation at executive levels is having women sponsor other women in their companies and in the community. My suggestion is that you not only look for sponsors to support you, but that in turn, you also sponsor women who are coming up the ranks behind you. This way, you can help them navigate the system and open doors whenever possible. You never know, with your help that young talent may shoot up the ladder and wind up helping you in the future.

What is an Advocate?

We all have a group of advocates. If you don't think you do, I invite you to browse the dozens of friends you have on your social networking pages. It's also likely you don't know half of your friends very well, but they may be more aware of you than you think.

An advocate could work at any level in the hierarchy ladder and is someone who speaks well of you in your presence and when you're not around. (And yes, a sponsor is also an advocate, but for clarity, I'd like to keep the two distinctions separate.) They're someone who admires and respects you and cooperates in building your reputation by commenting on your latest initiative or the opportunity you gave them. They may be the ones who point out to others how much you help the community or how you're always willing to help others with their projects. These individuals have enormous value in making your life easier. Typically they occupy assistant positions and are the ones who know everything that goes on in different departments, know the best time to approach your bosses to talk about certain issues, the cleverest strategy to get an appointment with someone or how to get invited to the event you're interested in.

As I mentioned in the previous chapter, advocates are as valid an ingredient in your network as are your sponsors and mentors. I've secured important contracts throughout my career thanks to someone I met at a conference and recommended me for a project. And I have plenty of examples of how low-ranking employees were key in advancing my projects and making sure everything ran smoothly. For example, after a college intern mentioned to the director of the student affairs department the impact that one of my books had on her, he hired me as a speaker; or the administrative assistant at a huge corporation I developed a nice relationship with and always made sure I received my checks on time; or the chief marketing officer's assistant, who, no matter how busy her boss was, always found a spot for me on her boss's schedule; or that young analyst who signed me up as a corporate trainer a few months after joining the company while that same company's diversity director claimed to never have enough money in the budget to bring me in; or that public relations assistant who constantly invites me to sit at her company's sponsored table at black-tie gala events.

It's easy to see why without this army of advocates it would be much harder for me to successfully do what I do. This group tends to receive little appreciation, yet if you conceptualize it as the oil that lubes the gears of your network, you'll change your attitude and devote well-deserved attention to them.

How to Find Advocates

This question is a bit less transparent than previous ones. It's as if I wanted to explain how to make friends. There is no one-size-fits-all recipe to follow and much will depend on your personality, the circle you move in, what you're looking for professionally, and other factors. On the other hand, there are also the advocates you'll never get to know. Yet I do follow a few principles that have worked well for me and I'd like to share them with you:

> ➤ Treat everybody nicely regardless of their rank. First, because all people deserve respect. Second, because you never know who knows who or when the recruiter who's interviewing you is using the assistant who asked you to fill out the form in the waiting room as their "ears." If you mistreat the assistant, you automatically close the door leading to the recruiter. Most people trust their administrative assistants and tend to protect them and take their opinions seriously. Third, because nowadays you never know who'll end up being your boss.

> ➤ Establish a personal relationship with assistants of high-ranking people you deal with or would like to deal with. Take an interest in their careers, their families, and aspirations. If at all possible, make your own contribution by narrowing the gap and helping them reach those dreams.

How to Handle the Relationship

It's hard to develop a personal relationship with advocates you don't know. In my case, it's with those who see me in the media or attend my conferences. Yet the principles I mentioned above apply equally to everyone. When I present I'm respectful of my audience's remarks or questions. I never dismiss someone else's opinion just because it differs from mine or because they lack a certain educational or professional level. This openness makes you more approachable, and therefore, nicer toward others.

Every now and then treat the advocates you know to something. Depending on the situation, it could either be a chocolate bar or a coffee, some flowers, or an invitation to participate at an event you have access to. We all like to be appreciated; even more so by people we admire. I also make it a point whenever I remember to send at least a quick greeting to people in my network that I know are my career advocates. I ask them what they've been up to or I send information on some relevant topic. Showing real interest is almost always the best way to build and keep long-lasting and productive relationships. It's not any different in this case.

What Is an Advisor?

The role of a mentor and advisor are easily confused. At times, the same person may serve both functions. An advisor may be an acquaintance, friend or colleague who knows you well and who you trust enough to inquire about specific topics you need help with.

Board of Advisors

Some years ago, when I decided to switch careers for the third time and start the journey I'm following now, I identified several people within my circle to advise me. Without realizing it I created my own board of advisors. This group works similarly to a company or organization's board of advisors. These are the people the CEO consults with about projects and ideas before putting them into practice. This enables listening to different points of view in order to make an educated decision.

The difference between my board and that of an organization's board of advisors is that in my case I don't meet them on a quarterly basis, and they are never together in the same room. Rather, I turn to them individually when I need to. The majority of my advisors are experts in certain areas. I have a producer friend who for years now has been advising me on my media appearances; a friend who provides advice on issues related to my work in corporations; a colleague who reviews all my educational books; another one who edits everything I write in English before publication, etc. Others are professionals and private coaches who get paid for services rendered: my agent, my lawyer, my manager, etc.

How to Find a Board of Advisors

The professional blend you'll need for your board will depend on the type of advice you're looking for. Some of my advisors were recommended to me by acquaintances, others I found through professional associations I belong to. Not only is it smart to join associations related to your industry to seek advisors, but in other industries where you can find experts that will prove useful. And only after establishing a trusted relationship with someone with a specialty that interests you should you begin consulting them on specific topics. The manner in which I typically connect with my advisors is informal. For example, if I'm preparing a segment on employment and I have a question, I call my executive recruiter colleague and consult with her. If I'm wondering how to approach a matter in the education field, I call my friend who holds three master's degrees in education.

What Is a Private Coach?

At some point in your career you'll need the services of an expert to help you navigate the inner workings of the business and corporate worlds. A private coach is an individual who is hired by you or the company you work for to guide you through a specific area you need work on. Whether it's on your company's dime or your own, having a coach who specializes in advancing middle management executives can make all the difference. Coaches are also especially helpful for individuals from lower social backgrounds or who were raised outside the U.S. where the rules are different.

In order to identify the type of coach you need, you must first assess your current situation and determine the areas you'd like to develop. Coaches can also be brought in from the outside to aid you in strengthening weak points or solving issues that are causing you stress in the office. (In the next chapter we'll talk in detail about the role of a coach in helping you solve conflicts in the workplace.) If you're fortunate, you may wind up at a company that automatically assigns coaches to their executives to help them master certain skills required for their position. Whether it's speaking to the media or negotiating in international markets, a coach can train you in a multitude of areas. If you are a business owner or need to hire your own coach, the best way to find the right one is to put out feelers through your professional network. Online groups with which you have an affinity are an obvious place to start.

With these new skills in your pocket, you'll climb that ladder even faster.

Chapter 11

To Err Is Human

Famous Women Speak: Anna María Chávez

In August 2011 the Girl Scouts of the United States (GSUSA) appointed Anna María Chávez as CEO. She is the first Latina to head the iconic organization which turned 100-years-old in 2012. Given that GSUSA is one of the premier leadership organizations for girls and young women, I felt it was extremely important to include her voice in a book for women. Before serving as Chief Executive of the Girl Scouts of Southwest Texas, Ms. Chávez, an attorney, had a long trajectory in public service. She was Senior Policy Advisor for U.S. Secretary of Transportation Rodney E. Slater, Chief of Staff for the Small Business Administration's Office of Government Contracting and Minority Enterprise Development, and more recently, Deputy Chief of Staff for urban relations and community development for former Arizona governor and current U.S. Secretary of Homeland Security, Janet Napolitano.

Q: *What kind of impact did being a young Girl Scout have on your life?*
A: I grew up in Eloy, Arizona, and became a Girl Scout at the age of ten. It had a powerful impact on my life. The experiences I had in Girl Scouting allowed me to begin thinking about opportunities beyond the city limits of my hometown. Through Girl Scouting, for instance, I had the opportunity to go to camp, which was the first time I'd ever traveled

anywhere without my family. Girl Scouting was one of the most formative experiences of my youth and I'm so privileged to serve today as
the organization's chief executive officer.

Q: *You left Phoenix to attend Yale University on a scholarship. That was a three-
thousand-mile trip away from home. What personal assets did you leverage
to have a fruitful college experience and what skills did you learn?*

A: I drew on courage, confidence, and character—the very skills we in
Girl Scouting seek to instill in girls today. I have also been blessed to
have incredible parents and a very supportive family and I've drawn
on that strength time and again in my life. I didn't know what to expect
when I arrived on the Yale campus all by myself. I was a small town kid
on scholarship, and I had to work two jobs to get by. I often tell the
story that one December, I was down to a dollar, a single dollar. I
thought, 'Anna, there's a lesson here, if you can just find it.' After all, Girl
Scouts had taught me to use resources wisely. I taped that dollar to
the wall over my desk so I'd know it was there—and if I spent it, I
wouldn't have anything at all. It got me through and I've kept drawing
on those lessons of resourcefulness and perseverance.

Q: *For several years you worked under a powerful woman, former Arizona governor Janet Napolitano. What was it like to have a female boss and in what way
was the experience different from having male bosses?*

A: I have been very fortunate to have wonderful male and female mentors throughout my career. Janet is certainly one of those people. She
is a wonderful leader and a great Girl Scout alumna. I also had the
privilege of working for former U.S. Secretary of Transportation Rodney
Slater and I learned a great deal from him. I find that each leader is
different, just as every person is different. I think the focus always has
to be on doing your very best and having a commitment to the vision
that has been laid out by a leader. I've always had a passion for public

service and both Janet and Rodney are extraordinary public servants, so I was fortunate to learn from the very best.

Q: *Given the demographic changes in this country, being the first Latina CEO of the Girl Scouts is very significant. What strategies can organizations and companies implement to increase the number of women and particularly diverse women in the top positions?*

A: This is so important. Diversity is a core value at Girl Scouting and has been from the beginning. We're very proud of that legacy. I think one of the key things that organizations or companies can do is to truly embrace diversity and inclusion. It's the right thing to do and it's good business. We've launched a cause campaign known as ToGetHer There.org or JuntosPorElla.org in Spanish, and the goal is to bring about balanced leadership across all sectors in a single generation by supporting and mentoring girls. So having organizations set up systems to mentor and sponsor women is also essential to filling that leadership pipeline.

Q: *Who have been some of the sponsors who have helped you in your career?*

A: I have to start with my parents. As I mentioned, I come from a very strong family and my mother was a great role model for me as a female elected official in Arizona at a time when there weren't that many of them. I also would highlight the amazing support of my teachers in high school and law school. As educators, they invested many hours to insure that I leveraged my skills and aptitude to reach my educational and professional goals.

Undoubtedly, we all make mistakes throughout our career trajectory. It's part of our experience as humans. And, if you're clever, you will transform these mistakes into opportunities to grow and gain expertise as a leader. But what happens when you make a serious mistake in the workplace? One of those mistakes where it seems there's no chance for recovery? The list of possible errors is endless, but here are a few: wrongly projecting your budget or sales; inappropriately estimating the time it would take to complete a project and failing to meet the deadline; losing it with a junior employee; making a mistake with your expenditure report; questioning your boss's authority in public; failing to report something someone told you that you should by law, and thousands of other possible goofs.

At times like this, many individuals of a diverse background may react with a blend of strong personal pride and an unclear understanding of how to manage conflicting situations within the corporate setting. And in the case of women, we must add that they typically take longer to ask for help in solving the mistake, making matters worse. These elements contribute to a seemingly insurmountable situation that can lead individuals to quit or lose their jobs followed by a prompt decision to drop their corporate careers and start working on their own.

And there's nothing wrong with choosing to be a self-employed businesswoman or professional; in fact, that's the road I chose as a writer and consultant. The point is to choose that path because you desire it and not because it's the only alternative when losing your job because you were unable to overcome a mistake. It's true that working for others can be a challenge and sometimes even frustrating. But if you don't have experience in being self-employed and decide to venture head-on in that direction as a reaction to what happened, chances are things won't go the way you expected them to.

If you can't solve your mistakes alone and can't seek advice from your support network (mentors and advisors), why not give yourself a real opportunity to achieve those desired goals by investing in a private coach to help you understand how company policy works in large corporations. This individual can help guide you through the steps you need to take to solve conflicts or mistakes made. In addition, this person can help explain how your own personality (including cultural traits) may be impacting the situation.

Some Typical Mistakes

At some point in your career you will experience conflict regardless of whether you work for someone, are self-employed or own a business. If you're aware of some of the most common stressful situations that can occur, you may be able to anticipate and act accordingly to either avoid them or manage them.

> ➤ When a project has a deadline, that date is nonnegotiable once the due date is established. Under certain circumstances you might be able to negotiate the deadline if you talk to your supervisors way ahead of time to give them, in turn, time to adjust their own dates. But don't think that your boss (or client) doesn't mention that date because he or she doesn't remember. As Ruth Gaviria says, "If your boss has to remind you of a deadline, then you're not doing your job." This issue of deadline noncompliance or the perception that deadlines are flexible is a complicated item for Latinos. It adds to the image of Latinos not having a sense of urgency and not taking their work seriously. As mentioned in previous chapters, it's crucial to adjust your notion of time to the U.S.'s if you wish to succeed in this country. It is also true if you wish to succeed in the global economy that tends to operate with Anglo-Saxon time parameters.

> ➤ And since we're talking about the difficulty of adjusting

to deadlines and the importance of adhering to the Anglo-Saxon timeframe, you must also avoid another mistake: arriving late to work or leaving earlier than your scheduled time. Anybody can have an emergency situation. But the red flags will go up when you make it a regular practice. Using any sort of excuse to justify not doing your job in the scheduled timeframe will put you in bad standing with your boss. The bottom line is that in today's competitive world there's little room for excuses. The best way to avoid being late is by including some slack time into your planning should any unforeseen problems arise. For example, if this manuscript is due on August 15, I know I must have it ready by July 30 because I don't know whether some of my writing may take longer or if I'll be especially busy with other commitments during the first two weeks in August. It's just like planning to go somewhere you know takes half an hour to get to. Ideally, you should add an extra fifteen minutes in case there's traffic. This way you'll be sure to get there on time.

➤ Another difficulty for individuals of our culture is controlling the amount of personal information we share with our coworkers. Knowing where to draw the line between being friends and having a friendly relationship is key in career advancement. While it's okay to share enough data for others to feel comfortable with you, it's also necessary to be prudent and not share too much information in order to prevent people from using it against you at some point.

➤ Not listening to your boss's feedback is pretty common, especially when such feedback is presented in a sandwich form. For instance, they start off with a positive statement, then talk about what you must improve on, and then close on a positive note: "Ana, I've noticed you've increased your participation during our team meetings this quarter. I think you should work on your communication style because sometimes you're too outspoken and that hinders effectiveness. But I believe your contribution during our meetings has been valuable and hope you continue along those lines." Unfortunately, many Latinos tend not to listen to the part that constitutes the meat in the sandwich, i.e., the part where the boss suggests improving Ana's communication style. So six months later, at her next performance review, Ana's boss will see no improvement and think she has no intention of changing her style. I know lots of people who were "surprised" when they were fired because they didn't take note of the important message between the two positive observations. That's why when your semiannual or quarterly review comes around, it's important to pay attention and explicitly ask about those areas your boss sees development opportunities in. Then be sure to work on them either alone or with the help of a coach.

➢ Remember that the impeccability of your word is a crucial part of your personal brand. Delivering on your promises and not backing out halfway into a task are the building blocks of your reputation. Sometimes, driven by the difficulty of turning someone down, you take on more than you can deliver. The problem is that once you start being known as someone who doesn't fulfill her promises, you're in big trouble. You'll lose credibility and other people's trust.

If you're ambitious and have a boss hindering your growth, the worst thing you could do is quit your job. I know many women who prefer to look for another job rather than face the situation and find a way out. This is the time to make good use of your mentors and private coaches in order to design a strategy enabling you to continue making progress without having your boss feel threatened by it.

Arturo Poiré says that one of the most common mistakes women make is not negotiating their hours in the workplace. "Latitude in the workplace must be a two-way street. For example, if you're a mom and your boss allows you to work from 8:00 AM to 4:00 PM, never volunteering for a project when your boss needs help because it entails staying later is unacceptable. But if you don't explain your situation and offer a Plan B such as, 'listen, I can't stay until 6:00 PM to finish the project because I must pick up the kids from school, but I can finish it later on from home,' your boss may take it that you're not a team player, that you're not interested in your job, or that you don't have the skill set to do it, etc. Yet, if you explain the truth and clarify that you're willing to do your part in a different timeframe, things will come off differently. Many women who have kids find it hard to give explanations but the truth is that they would benefit from being assertive because they'd be working just as hard as the rest. Many of them are online or connected to their Blackberries up to wee hours of the morning."

What to Do If You Make a Serious Mistake

Everyone, I insist, every single one of us makes mistakes. Some make them more often while others make more serious mistakes. And, obviously, as you grow in your career and take on more risks and responsibilities, the likelihood of committing a grave error increases. If you're in a managerial position, Ruth Gaviria has a few points worth considering.

THE VOICE OF EXPERIENCE

"In general, you must know that your chances for recovering from a serious mistake are greater than you think, if you're willing and keen to do what it takes to make amends. The secret is to acknowledge the mistake as soon as possible. If you find yourself experiencing the same situation two or three times, you must recognize it's your problem then and not theirs. You must examine what's happening and why you're acting in a way that proves detrimental to you."

—*Ruth Gaviria, Senior Vice President Corporate Marketing for Univision*

The question then is, when you've made one of those serious mistakes, what can you do to remedy the situation? Here are some steps that might help:

> ➢ Admit to yourself as soon as possible that you've made a mistake and don't assume the other person involved won't realize it. Burying your head in the sand is a terrible strategy. The other person may interpret that you're underestimating him/her which adds insult to injury.

> ➢ In our search to make sense of what happened we tend to build explanations to understand whose fault it was or justify our innocence or good intentions. The best thing to do is avoid wasting too much time discussing who was to blame and focus on solving the problem. Then look to see if any systemic causes could be fixed or understand the reason why someone (maybe you) let the ball drop. Admit to the other person that you've made a mistake, apologize and, if appropriate, ask how to best solve the situation.

> Set aside your ego and do whatever it takes to solve the problem. This is an important step to prove to yourself that you're ready to continue fighting for your dream and not to give it up.
> If it's serious enough, ask HR for advice in terms of learning the consequences of that mistake. If you're self-employed, you can consult with your mentors or advisors.
> If there's no one in your professional circle you can talk to about the issue, consider hiring a private coach for guidance.

If you hold a managerial or executive position, you should know that nowadays companies pretty often don't give their executives more than a couple of months' time to demonstrate their performance and productivity in a new position, which means they may fire you without having even made a mistake. This typically generates a high dose of angst. The best way to offset it is by building a team of internal and external advisors as soon as possible to help in the process of adapting to the workplace culture and what's expected of you. If there's a positive side to such high volatility, it's that the stigma felt in earlier days when being fired is quickly disappearing. Though this seems to apply more to higher ranking executives than it does for junior employees. This is not to say that you should behave as if the consequences don't faze you or that being fired isn't traumatic. But succumbing to the fear of "not being able to find another job if you're ever fired" is increasingly unrealistic.

Arturo Poiré's Corner
✦

"Careers are not a straight line toward success. You must always keep in mind what you've planned for because when you make a serious mistake you often forget what you once decided. And you must understand that lateral movements often allow you to disclose your whole potential. Sometimes moving up the ladder too soon may be counterproductive because you're not prepared for all that's required: technical knowledge, emotional and psychological maturity, and having the necessary expertise for that new position. All these elements must be in balance in order to move to the next level. Also, the more you progress in your career (move toward senior or executive positions) the less feedback you get from people. Everybody says yes and all's well to the CEO of a company. Messages become subtler, and so it's crucial to have a structure in place to get feedback, which may come from individuals enabled for such a purpose or via a coach whom you pay to point out mistakes."

PART THREE

Moving Ahead!
Plain Sailing

Chapter 12

It's Time to Say Yes to
Your Next Challenge

Famous Women Speak: María Celeste Arrarás

The attractive host and managing editor of Telemundo's "Al Rojo Vivo" practically needs no introduction. She started her career as a reporter in her native Puerto Rico, and she's been working in the U.S. since 1986. For many years, she cohosted Univision's successful news program "Primer Impacto." In 2005 she received an Emmy for her career achievements and the following year she was selected by *Newsweek* as one of "America's 20 Most Powerful Women." Whether in Spanish or English, her books are always hits (*Make Your Life Prime Time*, *Selena's Secret*, and *The Magic Cane*), and she's one of the most active celebrities on the Internet. One of her recent Twitcam chats reached eleven million people.

Q: *You've looked for challenges early on in life as an international swimming competitor. What drives you?*

A: I think that being an athlete since childhood encouraged me to be competitive, to search for excellence and set new goals every time I achieve previous ones. Since I was a child my father always encouraged me to swim and be a champion. He would say that eagerness to better yourself should come from within and that you must always strive to be better. I was also competitive academically speaking. I remember once coming home from school with a 'C' and my father strongly scolded me. He said, "Don't ever come into this house again with a 'C.' You either get an 'A' or an 'F.' You've got to be the best of the best or the best of the worst; anything but mediocre." That's a lifetime lesson I learned.

Q: *For many women it's hard to accept challenges when they don't feel 100% ready for such responsibility. What do you recommend to women who reject opportunities because they feel they don't have enough experience?*

A: I'd tell them to be brave enough to face their own fears. Life often places hurdles along the way . . . Why should we contribute to complicating matters by limiting ourselves? Of course we're all fearful of plunging into unknown challenges, but we must learn how to curb those fears. You grow when you learn how to surpass the limits of your comfort and safety zone. It's the only way to make meaningful progress. I don't allow myself to hesitate when faced with a challenge. I plunge into the water without much thought and I always rise to the surface. You always find a way to move ahead. You just need to foster faith in yourself.

Q: *How have you leveraged your Latina traits to be successful in the general American market and appear, for example, on NBC or the American Airlines channel produced by this same television station?*

A: I like to say that instead of crossover I do 'criss' crossover because I'm lucky enough to work in both markets simultaneously. It's wonderful to be able to navigate these two completely different worlds; I learn how to understand both audiences, and it's a self-learning process as well. I never leveraged the fact that I was Latina to work in English-language television. But once I was offered the opportunity, it was very clear to me that I couldn't fake what I was not. I'm Latina in my gestures, my accent, and my personality. I've never really tapped into the fact but neither have I minimized it.

Q: *On a scale from 1 to 5 (1 being the lowest) do you consider yourself:*

a. Risk taker: 4
b. Competitive: 5
c. Ambitious: 3

A: My conclusion is that in order to be competitive you must be willing to take risks. The competitive individual, however, takes on very heavy risks. The danger with ambition is that it forces you to undertake unnecessary risks.

In 2011, Facebook's chief operating officer Sheryl Sandberg delivered the keynote address at Barnard College's commencement ceremony. When I interviewed Debora Spar, president of the renowned women's college within Columbia University, I asked what advice she would give a woman who is midway into her career. She quoted Sheryl's words from her commencement speech at Bard. I had seen it via YouTube and these words had also sparked my attention: "Do not lean back; lean in. Put your foot on that gas pedal and keep it there until the day you have to make a decision, and then make a decision. That's the only way, when that day comes, you'll even have a decision to make."

Sheryl was referring to the fact that women make decisions too early in their career based on future wishes that are years away from materializing. For example, a recent college graduate in her twenties decides not to accept a job because it entails traveling. She's thinking a few years down the road that she'll want to have kids and it'll be hard to travel then. Consequently, she rejects the opportunity, yet she doesn't even have a boyfriend! That's what Facebook's COO was suggesting. Instead of projecting ten steps ahead, accept that promotion and when the time is right to have children, decide otherwise. Meanwhile, continue advancing in your career and don't get stuck with some plan you won't be putting into practice for many more years to come. Bearing this in mind, it's high time you asked yourself what you can do to expand the opportunities that appear before you. Consider how you can achieve greater visibility so that executives and other powerful individuals can identify you and offer you those opportunities.

When my first book came out, *How to Find a Job in the U.S.*, I was faced with a dilemma. I was interested in doing workshops on this topic but given the nature of the subject, I used to get constant requests to present in exchange for very little compensation or pro bono in community organizations and libraries. And although I would have wanted to help everybody, the truth is I had to earn money to pay the bills; I wouldn't have been able to build my business if I had donated all of my time. So I decided to invest my time doing pro bono television and radio segments. This enabled me to gain visibility faster and, in turn, a larger audience could benefit from my advice. Another goal was also met: clients came knocking on my door because they had seen me on television, instead of me having to go out looking for clients.

The same applies whether you work for a company or are self-employed. When senior employees (or potential clients) see and like what you do, they will contact you. If they don't see you, or don't know you're behind some particular achievement, it's highly unlikely they'll call you. So, observe your current situation, and, focusing your attention on your intention, try to align certain activities to achieve greater visibility and add value to your talent and the society at large. At times, your community work is what makes you more relevant to your company; at others, it's what you do within the company in areas not directly related to your daily responsibilities. And if you're thinking, 'Oh, my god, I'll have to work even harder now?' The answer is yes and no. It's yes because if you're not including some of the activities I shared with you here, it's likely you're not tapping into the possibilities of others noticing you. And it's also no because the idea is to focus on your results and not necessarily on working more hours.

How to Get Started

There are several strategies for ensuring your work, talent, and potential are noticed by others. Whatever combination of distinct strategies you decide to implement will relate to your goals, style, and the time latitude you may have.

Presenting

We've already discussed the importance of being an active team member and participant in large group meetings in order to build your reputation. We also mentioned the importance of making your opinions heard and being able to express disagreement with others through legitimate arguments. To expand your brand beyond your company, presenting at conferences and special events is one of the strategies I find most productive.

Before booking yourself to speak in front of a large audience, I strongly suggest preparing yourself for it first. Speaking in public could be a stressful experience for many people, and if you get it wrong, you'll be doing yourself a disservice. The idea is to start off speaking before small groups and gradually increase the size of your audience as you gain confidence in yourself. Consider presenting at a local high school or college where you can inspire students to continue with their studies, or talk about your profession which will enable you to gain experience without losing face before your colleagues. To develop your skills as a public speaker, you could also opt for becoming a member of your local Toastmasters International group (www.toastmasters.org). You'll receive basic training, practice time, and gentle feedback to help improve your performance.

If you're an introvert or shy, or if you simply don't like the idea of presenting in public, webinars (seminars via the Internet) can be a good alternative. This way you can be alone in front of the computer, and though one of the options is for the audience to be able to see you, you can't see them. And since these seminars can be filed, they enable you to share your knowledge, experience, and points of view with a large number of people without having to be physically present.

Where to Present

You'll have plenty of opportunities to present. My suggestion is not to present for the sake of presenting but strategically choose what conferences or internal and external events are worth appearing at. In doing so, it's always timely to ask yourself:

- ➤ Which audience do I want to benefit?
- ➤ What kind of audience do I want to target?
- ➤ Who organizes the event and what's their reputation?
- ➤ What's the cost/benefit of this particular event?

If you have your planning sheets with your goals in front of you, it'll be easier to answer these questions because the answer to each depends on your goal. For instance, if you're a finance expert but your goal is to be invited to participate in your company's diversity and inclusion board because you believe such work will provide visibility, perhaps it's best to consider presenting at diversity and inclusion conferences where HR and talent development managers and executives from your company will also be present. Not only will you get to meet a few key players there, but, more importantly, they'll have a chance to notice you. And if you do a good job, that tilts the scale toward you.

However, given the amount of conferences available in each specialty, it's not a bad idea to explore which are more reputable and which are not well organized. The latter is worth researching because if they don't comply with scheduled timetables, it also probably means that their invited speakers tend not to show up and it could be a waste of your time and money. These types of events don't attract the best quality people since rumors spread fast and people stop going. It's best to use your network for conference recommendations worth participating in.

How to Participate

I'd say the easiest way to start is by offering to present at events organized by your own company or organization. If you run your own business or work in a small company, explore opportunities with small or midsized nonprofit organizations, as well as school districts or universities that organize professional career sessions to inspire students. Also be sure to contact your local chamber of commerce and the local chapters of professional organizations you can become a member of.

Some conferences issue RFPs (Request for Proposals), which are requests for presentation proposals that are assessed by a committee. These are typically the most competitive conferences and sometimes politics come into play because sponsors' presentations must be prioritized. At others, you may only be able to present if your company sponsors the event. And yet at others, if you know the organizers, you might suggest a relevant topic. This also happens at smaller or local conferences where good pro bono speakers are needed. If the right audience is present, it may be a perfect starting point.

As usual, the best way to make the connection is through your network. Who might you know that can recommend you to present at the conference you're interested in? And if you still don't know anybody, focus your attention on developing contacts active in the conference circuit. Your social media can work magic in this case.

Leading Employee Groups and Other Committees

When I talk to high school or college students I always insist that no matter what type of team, club or organization they belong to they should never be mere participants but assume leadership roles.

The same happens professionally. Leaders of any type of organization are individuals with high exposure levels: their names appear in board meeting minutes, in emails, and other communications. And due to their daily work activities they acquire knowledge in multiple areas since they're in contact with executives and know speakers and sponsors (for our purposes here, individuals who contribute funds to events) who are invited to their conferences.

In large companies, it's become increasingly common to find employee groups that go by names such as: Employee Resource Group (ERG), Employee Business Group (EBG), and Employee Network, etc. Setting aside distinctive details, almost all aim to recruit, retain, and develop their employees. Some create a space where those belonging to the same affiliation (race, ethnic background, sexual orientation, generation, etc.) feel comfortable and can be heard. In recent years, partly driven by the financial crisis in 2008, there's been an increased need for these groups to assist in generating business for the consumer group they represent.

For instance, a company's Latino employees could help adapt products or ad campaigns for the Hispanic market. A few years ago, the Hispanic employee group at American Express helped design a Christmas gift called *Felicidades*. Instead of featuring the typical American Express logo for the holidays, the card contained a colorful illustration and message directed at their Hispanic customers. Another example: the women's group at Marsh (WEBB), one of the largest insurance and risk advice organizations worldwide, organizes events at Saks Fifth Avenue and invites clients and prospects to socialize and shop with discount coupons at the department store closed exclusively for them. They use these events—there's always a guest speaker and top executives on the guest list—to reinforce the relationship with their clients, while generating a great deal of new business.

Joining a group like this is ideal for acquiring more visibility. First, because there's almost always an executive acting as a sponsor (here, an individual who opens doors and puts his/her reputation on the line for his/her protégés), and, second, because typically they report to the diversity and inclusion department, i.e., you get visibility in a department that's always looking for high potential diverse talent to promote. I know many women (and men) who, because of these periodic group meetings with executives, have developed close relationships with their CEOs as a result. And since strong bonds are generated between current and past leaders, between leaders of different groups, and even employee groups from different companies, being part of such a group will expand your network. Currently, there are employee group consortiums in cities like Chicago and New York that meet regularly. Being a part of these groups exponentially multiplies your access to both in-company as well as external opportunities.

If employee groups don't exist in your company, or if you work for a small business, then create your own type of event. You can produce seminars, galas, luncheons, or conferences, and place yourself at the head of the organizing committee. This is always a smart option if you're a businesswoman. Supporting a cause you're interested in through a fund raising event not only provides visibility, it also enables you to connect to other like-minded individuals. As part of the Red Shoe Movement, we have a large network of ambassadors who help organize and run events across the country. They not only have access to a strong network of individuals who work in a wide range of industries, but to dynamic event speakers and participants. If you opt for partnering with other small businesses, you'll multiply the effect of your efforts. The formula for success remains the same: if you're in an organization, try to assume a leadership role instead of simply being a participant.

Many women (Latinas especially) ask themselves if it's worth getting involved in yet another activity that'll take them away from their families. To many, the answer is no. For example, Carla Dodds from Walmart U.S. says, "We women have so many roles; we have work and family and being on the board is yet another thing to add to the list. I was asked to be the director of an employee group, but at the end of the day I don't want to commit to serve in an organization if I can't devote appropriate time to it. I believe that when my son starts college I'll be more willing to participate."

Like all things in life, everything depends on your situation and what you want to achieve. What's important is not to ignore the fact that these organizations open doors and enable you to expand your brand's impact. If you can find the time at some point in your career to join them, it will be worth the sacrifice.

Become a Mentor and Support Others

Now that you know what a mentor, sponsor, advocate, and advisor can do to help advance your career (see chapter ten), I'd like you to now think about how you can play a similar role in someone else's life.

You're probably already aware that this book aims not only to help you in your journey, but to prepare you to help others who are coming up behind you. While writing this book I learn from my interviewees as I teach my readers. It's always a chain. Someone helps me move one step ahead and I stretch my arm out to help the one behind me. The problem is that this chain can often break, leaving us hanging, without anyone to lend us a hand or explain how to go to the next level. Without anyone introducing us to the right person or suggesting our name when discussing a possible promotion, you're left completely on your own.

Unfortunately, the ones who frequently break that support chain are other women. I invite you not to be one of them. I urge you not to believe that if you help other women, there'll be less in it for you, or to think that in your company or industry there's only room for a limited number of women. This mindset impacts you as well as our gender. Instead of expanding possibilities for all of us, it reduces them. It's much more productive to think that the more women in decision-making positions there are, the more natural it'll be to see them in such positions and the better it'll be for us all. You'll notice that once this thought settles in your mind, your actions will align to it and you'll begin to see different results for the women around you.

To encourage you to take on this challenge with the same determination you would apply to seeking your own mentors, sponsors, etc., I've included a space below where you can write down the names of the women you'll be helping and the role you'll be playing in their lives. Ideally, the list should include each of the women you're related to professionally and the current role you play in their careers. You can then project the role you'd like to play in the future. For example, right now my relationship with Sandra is being her informal mentor. In the future I'd like to be her sponsor. Or, currently my relationship with Andrea is neutral. We're colleagues and nothing else. In the future I'd like to be more actively involved as her advocate. The point is to decide what actions I must take to materialize that new role. In Sandra's case, I can start talking about her with other executives I know and suggest her for a project that implies a professional challenge. In terms of Andrea, I can talk about her with other colleagues and spread the word through my social networks about her achievements.

Name	My current relationship is					In the future I'll be				
	N	M	S	A	A	N	M	S	A	A

N = Neutral; M = Mentor; S = Sponsor; A = Advocate; A = Advisor

Though it may seem odd, helping other women is not just a way of paying back what others have done for you, it also increases your relevance and visibility. For one, the people you advise, counsel, guide, and open doors for become advocates who will continue building your reputation. By supporting other women's projects and sponsoring their groups you're also sending a clear leadership message to your company's executives. Lending a hand to women is not just something we all must morally do but also something which in the long run will benefit us in multiple ways.

Accept Projects That Imply Some Challenge

As mentioned in earlier chapters, women tend to be extremely cautious and prefer not to give their opinions until they fully understand a subject. The reluctance and fear of saying something wrong or assuming a role you're not prepared for may be related to those early mandates received which point to the fact that you must be perfect. These mandates suggest that the margin of error for women is much smaller than for men; a reality that's often confirmed in the news when high-level female executives are dismissed from their jobs for making mistakes which are otherwise tolerated in men.

The point is that successful women—those who move ahead in their field—tune out those fears and embrace challenges even when they're not 100% ready. For instance, Gloria Ysasi-Díaz, Vice President of Grainger Supply Chain says, "Early on I took on assignments where 70% or 80% was unknown. Now, with all these years of experience, I typically know 50% of what I'll be doing when I accept a new project."

For women like Gloria, not knowing an important percentage of what they'll be doing in a new position is the most exciting part: they love the challenge and resort to their creativity, inner resources, and people around them to fill in the gaps. Essentially, the only way to grow professionally is being open to opportunities where you can acquire new knowledge or skills, or where you can fine-tune existing ones. Explore new environments and don't allow those mandates planted by others in your subconscious early on in life hold you back from your desires.

THE VOICE OF EXPERIENCE

"Throughout my career I held jobs I wasn't 100% prepared for. Maybe I knew 30% of what I had to do but I also knew that with effort and dedication I would advance and learn the remaining 70% I needed to become successful. I think it has to do with Argentine culture which taught me to be bold and to have some nerve in order to survive. And also a positive mindset to think where there's a will there's a way. Of course I wouldn't rush into something I know nothing about or get involved in rocket science because I'm not a scientist. But if it's somehow related to business, requiring some skill sets I do have, then I most certainly accept the challenge. If you're working in a team and your experience is limited, it's extremely important to communicate your level of expertise with absolute transparency, and also express your willingness to learn. Women naturally focus more on details; they're more cautious. They need everything to be perfect before taking risks. They're able to estimate multiple ways in which something may turn out, to the extent of delaying action or not even taking action. In my opinion, such perfectionism often plays against us. We should try to be less exact and use our capacity to see details within those risks we're willing to take."

—*Carla Dodds, Senior Director for Marketing*
Retail Formats, Walmart Brazil

In the U.S. (as well as in the rest of the world) the best way to move ahead is by getting involved in increasingly more complex projects, and assuming positions of greater responsibility. If you always do what you've always done or what's easiest or most comfortable, it's likely that your career will come to a standstill. Besides, nowadays, if you don't make progress, you run the risk of not being able to remain in the same position and eventually be fired. In such a competitive global economy, no matter what size company you're in, employers look for the best employees, those that are creative, problem-solvers, and who readily offer their help to complete a project in record time. If you're self-employed, you'll face the same situation. If you're not after new business opportunities, if you don't adopt new technologies, or if you won't accept doing a task you're not 100% familiar with, your clients will find someone who will.

So, just as I'm suggesting you give your opinion even if you haven't earned a Ph.D. on the subject, I also invite you to accept that project your boss proposed which requires studying a new program and finding yourself a mentor to guide you through the process. Remember, if you reject these proposals and promotions, the chances are slim they'll offer one to you again. You'll wind up dropping from the high potential category to the group that's not ready to go to the next level.

Accept Lateral Movements

At times, the best way to revitalize your career is to train in a different area. Whether it's some aspect of your industry unknown to you, a new role, a different market or a department change. These types of changes are often coupled with some lateral movement. As Arturo explains in one of his corners, it's a natural part of the journey you transit through in your career.

THE VOICE OF EXPERIENCE

"It's preferable to make mistakes in market number sixty-five than in market number one [with the largest audience] because it implies less repercussion and people forgive your mistakes more readily. For example, if you're a news producer in New York and want to become a news director, first accept the job as news director in South Carolina, acquire the skill sets there, learn all you have to learn and, in due time, you'll be able to go back to New York."

—*Catherine McKenzie, Senior Producer for ABC's*
"Good Morning America"

It's best to always be alert and not let opportunities slip by just because they entail moving to a smaller city for a time or learning a new skill set. These movements may help you find an unknown niche in your industry where your skills are valued.

As a female born into Latino culture, you mustn't lose sight of the fact that if you don't have a clear career plan, accepting lateral movements may sometimes become a habit that may move you away from your goals. Given Latinos' characteristic flexibility, our loyalty to our colleagues, and our difficulty with saying no, it may be hard to reject your boss's offer to assume a role that doesn't advance your goals. That's why it's important to assess each offer and talk it over with your mentors and advisors. This way you'll be able to estimate the short- and long-term effects of accepting that lateral move.

Continue Studying

In recent years I've seen several friends and colleagues go back to school. One friend received a Ph.D. in education from Harvard University; another, her third master's degree in education; a third earned a master's degree in museum administration; another an MBA, and yet another a master's degree in digital design. Three of these cases are mothers with three children. Evidently, finding time to study was a real sacrifice for them. Yet, they knew that to grow in their professions they needed an additional degree.

If you feel you're at a standstill at work, or that your daily routine bores you because it's below your capacity level or because it's just not interesting enough, consider going back to college. For one, certain positions require a master's degree. It's also a good way of getting a salary increase since the majority of companies recognize your efforts with money. In addition, it could be an effective way of changing your role or even industry. Let's suppose you have a degree in engineering and work as a systems engineer in a communications company. Having an MBA may allow you to access a managerial position at any company where your training as an engineer, along with your ability to see the overall picture, is appreciated. In addition, depending on the size of the company, they may even pay for your studies. So, keep doing the research. There are plenty of one-year MBA programs available and companies that will pay tuition for their high-potential employees.

In the case of Latinas, though more of us are graduating from college than Hispanic men, there are still too few of us with advanced degrees, and this impacts our participation in high-power positions. It's therefore critical for you not only to continue with your studies but also to instill this continued education philosophy in your daughters and other women you're in contact with.

Most certainly, before rushing into a master's program it's a good idea to estimate the real impact it'll have on your work opportunities. I was recently contacted by a fifty-five-year-old woman who has worked her entire life in the banking sector and earned a degree in that field. Two years ago she lost her job and was struggling to find another one although she'd been to dozens of interviews. During her interviews she was told that it was a shame she didn't have a master's degree. She believes her best option is to get one (although she has no money to pay for her studies), and then switch to the health industry which offers more job opportunities. The truth is that at her age, she probably won't be able to get a return on her investment in a master's degree, especially because she wants to start in a new field and with no experience.

If you're in a similar situation, the best bet for revitalizing your career is to take short courses, learn a new discipline, and add technical skills or leadership examples to your knowledge toolbox.

THE VOICE OF EXPERIENCE

"You just don't realize how hard it is to jump from the intermediate to the executive level. There are less available positions and the process itself takes a long time. This means you must keep in touch with people who interview you and be patient. The higher you go up the ladder, the longer the decision-making process. Nobody tells you that in order to hire a vice president many people will be interviewed; candidates go onto a second and third interview and then a group meets to talk about those candidates. The whole process takes months. It's not like being interviewed for a more junior position where you can expect an answer in two-week's time."

—*Catherine McKenzie, Senior Producer for ABC's*
"Good Morning America"

Chapter 13

The Power Is in Your Hands

We've come a long way together through the pages of this book. During the process, I hope you were able to achieve the following:

> **1.** Discover your dream and where it falls on your priority list.

> **2.** Identify old mandates that impact your self-esteem and your verbal and nonverbal messages.

> **3.** Learn what success means to you and establish career goals that align with your own definition of success.

> **4.** Incorporate new tools and strategies to your plan so you can tread the path firmly.

> **5.** Understand that without sacrificing who you are, you can modulate your personality traits according to the situation in order to prioritize your goals.

I'd like to remind you what Arturo said in an earlier chapter: At times, being aware of what you want may be both stimulating and frustrating. For one, it's wonderful to discover what your wishes are (versus wishes others have in store for you) and be able to organize your actions to get closer to them. Yet, when you finally discover what really satisfies you, what moves you and makes you feel alive, you're suddenly assaulted by frustration for all the lost time. This could too quickly turn into a desperate need to obtain your goals *this minute*. If that's the feeling you're left with after reading this book, take a few moments to think about my initial advice: Life is a journey, not a race toward a destination. Your career is also a journey, and as such, you must enjoy each stage, including this one, where you may have discovered what you yearn for, or what you didn't know you needed in order to achieve your goals. Nothing you've done so far is wrong. From now on you'll have tools and distinctions you lacked before you started this journey. (The same is true for any nonfiction book you read, course you enroll in or when you have one of those revealing talks with your mentor.)

You do what you can, whenever you can, and with whatever you have at hand. Not all of us are ready to grow at the same pace, in the same way or using the same methods. We don't all seek to achieve the same results either. That's why I insist on the fact that *your* journey is absolutely unique. You will now walk in your own red shoes, so avoid treading on paths others have chosen for you. That's why I suggested taking what is useful from my interviewees' stories and personal experiences and adapting those to your own particular situation, without falling into narratives like, "I should've done this or that."

Each of us comes equipped with assets from our own cultural and educational backgrounds, as well as with our own needs and emotions. When you incorporate new resources into your everyday routine, new opportunities open up. Yet *you* are the one who decides what to take in and when. *You* decide when to move ahead and when to accept a lateral position that will allow you to grow in a certain area. *You* decide how much to follow others' suggestions and the extent to which to listen to your own voice.

If you feel you're ready now and that you've found the way to fulfill your goals, do not despair. Plan your journey with the tools you've discovered in this book and you'll see that sooner than you imagined (but probably a little later than what your anxiety cries out for) you'll attain the success you deserve.

Good luck on your journey!

Epilogue

As I was finishing this book, the very reputable business magazine *Crain's New York Business* published a list of the "50 Most Powerful Women in New York." There wasn't a single Latina on that list. Forty-seven women were Anglo-Saxon; one was African American; one Chinese American, and one Indian American.

I decided to send a letter to the editor as I've been doing for quite some time now. This time I took it to a different level. Since I'm tired of not receiving responses to these types of letters, I wrote about it for my blog. Then I posted a copy of the letter on all my social networks and emailed my media acquaintances. Fox News Latino asked me to write an exclusive column for them that had such visibility I received calls from several television programs, including two CNN shows, to speak about the *Crain's* feature.

The way I see it is that editors (the majority white males) who make up these lists have a very homogeneous network. Therefore, the majority of recommendations they receive for the list come from other Anglo-Saxons. If you examine your own network and who's in it, a great percentage is likely to be Latinas who know other Latinos. If you live in Latin America, it's likely that your network will comprise people from your own country, your same social class, or even your same city, province or state.

The habit of socializing mostly with individuals from our own ethnic and racial group is not exclusive to Anglo-Saxons. We all tend to do the same because it's the easiest or most comfortable way to go about it. That's why Latinas and women from groups not represented on that list are also partly responsible for not making themselves known in Anglo-Saxon power circles. The more we continue presenting within our own groups and affiliating exclusively with members of our own tribe, the less we will be able to expand our sphere of influence.

By the same token, Latino publications come up with their own lists of the most influential Latinas. But this list divide implies that Latinas only influence and lead other Latinas and not the society at large. Yet, it's easy to see that Carolina Herrera's designs are appreciated by women of all races and ethnic backgrounds; the U.S. Secretary of Labor, Hilda Solís, has power over domestic labor policy, and that Supreme Court Justice Sonia Sotomayor's votes have a bearing on the laws governing the country.

For many people these lists are frivolous, inconsequential or stage-managed; and more than one is. Yet, those who appear on such lists get free publicity and then use the fact of having appeared on them to promote their companies and careers. This type of press attracts more opportunities, and, therefore, more visibility. Although you may think that people are on those lists through contacts—in many cases it's absolutely true—you too can go after those contacts. By doing so, the influential editors and producers who create such lists will know about your work and include you on them if you deserve it.

The other serious problem I see with Latinas not appearing on mainstream lists is that it sends out the message that there are no qualified Latinas to include. And this is far from true. The fact that editors aren't aware of them doesn't mean they don't exist. Yet, when millions of readers read those fifty names, see photos and don't see any diversity, the immediate conclusion is: Well, there probably is no Latina leader in New York.

As I mentioned in the chapter "Networking, That Miracle Word," it's not easy to abandon the circles we're used to in order to penetrate new ones. I find it difficult sometimes to convince mainstream media producers that not only Latinos are interested in these topics. But if we don't keep trying, we'll continue having conversations that don't achieve the widespread impact they could otherwise have. I also find it hard to be invited to present at general conferences, and not just those on occupational diversity. Or to be invited to talk about any subject—career development, women in the labor market, etc.—that doesn't have to do with Latino topics. The fact that I'm Latina is beneficial because my viewpoint will be different from non-Latino presenters, but it doesn't mean that I can *only* talk about topics that interest this group.

I make an effort to avoid self-segregating myself. And I invite you to consider doing the same in your search for expanding your sphere of power and influence. It is high time we assume the responsibility we each have for our career, the progress of other women, and the Hispanic community both in the U.S. as well as in the rest of the world. Latinas have a very important role to play in this new challenge. What are we waiting for?

The Red Shoe Movement

When the Spanish-language edition of this book came out I launched the Red Shoe Movement (RSM), a movement to help increase female representation at executive levels in all types of organizations which invites women to wear red shoes on Tuesdays to signal their support. The idea, at the crossroads of fashion and empowerment, took off faster than I had imagined. I immediately started receiving messages from women across the U.S., Latin America, Europe and Asia asking what they needed to do to bring the movement to their towns. It was obvious to me that a lot of these women were ready to help others reach their career aspirations.

It's a simple concept: when women open doors for each other there's one less hurdle in the way. The more accustomed we become to seeing women in high-ranking jobs, the more opportunities there will be for all of us. Wearing red shoes invites other women to approach you, it reminds you of what you stand for, and it keeps the conversation about parity in the workplace going. So, at any given point if you feel a pang of jealousy or a "why she and not me" when a colleague gets praised or promoted, your red shoes will rescue you and recommit you to your goal of supporting your gender-mates.

Start a Red Shoe Book Club
This is an ideal book to read with a group of friends or colleagues so you can identify any old mandates that might still be holding you back. It can help you recognize the dreams you have for your-

self (as opposed to those that other people had for you), determine what success means for you, develop your personal brand, strengthen your network, and work on a lot of other areas that are critical if you want to advance in your career.

As you share personal information and ask for honest feedback, group members grow closer, and soon, what started as a weekly or bi-weekly book club, will naturally become an advisory board. That's when you can take your club to the next level.

Create Your Own Red Shoe Support Network

Once you've formed a group you can strategize on how to extend your help to other women in your organization, support the growth of one individual member at a time, create large events, invite speakers to cover specific issues, become mentors of younger women and girls, and so on. You can either chose to start a support network with your colleagues at work or with that special group of girlfriends who have always been there for you to provide feedback and cheer you along.

What's Next

By the time this book is published, the movement will have grown and evolved even further. We're already hard at work creating chapters that will operate independently. I hope you join the movement as a participant, as an ambassador or as a chapter leader. It's time to start playing an active role in bringing more women to decision-making positions. Please post your pictures and stories on the Red Shoe Movement Facebook page so we can all take part in your success.

www.RedShoeMovement.com
www.facebook.com/RedShoeMovement
Connect with us via: info@redshoemovement.com

Acknowledgments

I wrote this book in record time to meet my editor's deadline. This was possible thanks to the help of a great number of people. I'd like to start by thanking my two assistants Cristina Pinzón and Irma Encarnación, and the people who so generously shared their experiences with me: Miguel Alemañy, Midy Aponte, Daisy Auger-Domínguez, Terri Austin, Lucía Ballas-Traynor, Melissa Bee, George E. Borst, Jazmin Cameron, Vikki Campos, Martina Caracoche, Gilberta Caron, Martha Alicia Chávez Martínez, Juana Cruz Tollinchi, Carla Dodds, Esther R. Dyer, John Edwardson, Miriam Fabiancic, Mariel Fiori, Carol Franks-Randall, Ruth Gaviria, Liliana Gil, Anna Giraldo-Kerr, Rebeca Gómez Palacio, Michael P. Howard, Diane Librizzi, Susan Landon, Shirley Limongi, Frank Marrero, Catherine McKenzie, Christine Mendonça, Lina Meruane, Elizabeth Nieto, Miguel R. Olivas-Luján, Laureeen Ong, John Pout, Gloria Puentes, Beatriz Quezada, Shubha Ramaswamy, Michael I. Roth, Pamela Ravare-Jones, Will Robalino, Debora Spar, Michell Tollinchi-Michel, John B. Veihmeyer, Cristina Vilella, Blanca Rosa Vilchez, Janet Wigfield, and Gloria Ysasi-Diaz.

I wish to especially thank María Celeste Arrarás, Ivonne Baki, Carolina Bayón, Nora Bulnes, María Antonieta Collins, Remedios Díaz Oliver, Anna María Chávez, Nancy Dubuc, Dra. Aliza Lifshitz, Elvira Lindo, María Marín, Soledad O'Brien, Elena Poniatowska, Elena Roger, María Elena Salinas, Roselyn Sánchez, and

Cristina Saralegui for being so open and sharing their experiences on their path to fame and success. And my gratitude to Beatriz Parga, Augusta Silva, Leylha Ahuile, Frank Marrero, Marcela Álvarez, and Elaine King for making the interviews in this book possible.

I am deeply indebted to those who read the manuscript and guided me in specific areas: my sister, Paula Dabbah, and Ingrid Ellicker, both psychoanalysts. I owe much to Arturo Poiré and Elizabeth Nieto who took on the task of reading the manuscript to provide their feedback. I know how burdensome this responsibility is and I thank you both for taking the trouble to do it. Thank you Arturo Poiré for indulging us with your powerful imprint through "Arturo's corners."

I would like to thank my friend Karen Tawil for translating this book into English. She accepted the challenge lovingly, with great professionalism and worked against the clock. Thanks to Adriana V. López for her impeccable editing of this English-language edition. Your attention to detail is amazing and I look forward to continue working with you in the future. I wish to thank my agent James Fitzgerald for trusting me, my publishers, Carlos Azula and Erik Riesenberg, for their enthusiasm and support, and Andrea Montejo for her careful editing of the original book written in Spanish.

Finally, I would like to acknowledge Teresa Correa for implementing the first Red Shoe Book Club in the country at Avon. She has become the Head Brand Ambassador of the Red Shoe Movement and a powerful source of inspiration to thousands of women. To her and to our wonderful team of ambassadors, my deepest gratitude.